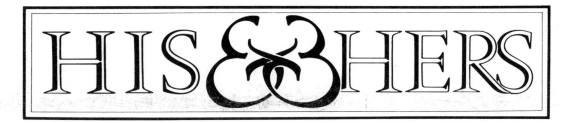

Also by Stanley Marcus

Minding the Store
Quest for the Best

S·T·A·N·L·E·Y M·A·R·C·U·S

THE VIKING PRESS·NEW YORK

HIS
&
HERS

·THE·
F·A·N·T·A·S·Y
W·O·R·L·D
OF
THE *Neiman-Marcus*
C·A·T·A·L·O·G·U·E

To the Memory of
EDWARD MARCUS,
*who led Neiman-Marcus into the
land of mail order*

First published in 1982 by The Viking Press
625 Madison Avenue, New York, N.Y. 10022
Published simultaneously in Canada by
Penguin Books Canada Limited

LIBRARY OF CONGRESS CATALOGING IN PUBLICATION DATA
Marcus, Stanley, 1905–
    His and hers.
    1. Neiman-Marcus.   2. Catalogs, Commercial—Texas.
3. Mail-order business—Texas.   I. Title.
HF5465.U6N45   1982   381′.14′09764   82-70129
ISBN 0-670-37263-3   AACR2

The photograph of Stanley Marcus on page 7
was taken by Shelly Katz.

Grateful acknowledgment is made to the following
for permission to reprint copyrighted material:
Erma Bombeck and Field Newspaper Syndicate: "Life Size
Dummies Make Christmas Wish," by Erma Bombeck, *The Clarion-
Ledger,* Jackson, Mississippi, October 24, 1972. Used by permission.
The Miami Herald: "Is Ark a Lark? 'Perfect Retreat'
Costs $588,247," by Mike Baxter, *The Miami Herald,*
Miami, Florida, October 27, 1970. Used by permission.

The Neiman-Marcus logo is reproduced by permission
of Neiman-Marcus.

Printed in the United States of America
Set in Century Schoolbook and Futura Light
Designed by Gael Towey Dillon

WE GRATEFULLY ACKNOWLEDGE PERMISSION TO
REPRODUCE NEIMAN-MARCUS CATALOGUE COVERS ON
THE FOLLOWING PAGES:

48, by Elsie Shaver, 1942; 50 (top), 50 (bottom), by Marcel
Vertés, 1943, 1945; 52, 53, by Madeleine Pilgreen-
Treadgold, 1947, 1949; cover and envelope on pages 56–57,
by Saul Steinberg, 1951; 60, 62, 70–71, by Ann B. Pearle,
1952, 1953, 1957; 63, by Renée Forsyth, 1954; 64–65, by
Ludwig Bemelmans, 1955; 85, by Ronald Searle, 1961;
93, 148, by Björn Wiinblad, 1963, 1973, copyright by
Signature AG, Glarus, Switzerland; 100, 123, by Ib Antoni,
1964, 1969; 106–107, by Ben Shahn, 1966, copyright © by
the Estate of Ben Shahn; 118–19, by Robert Indiana, 1968;
133, by Karen Nelson, 1970; 142, by Victor Vasarely, 1972,
courtesy S.P.A.D.E.M., Paris; 160–61, by Mark Tobey,
1975, by permission of Trans World Art Corp., N.Y.C.;
cover illustration for 1976, on page 169, from the Laurice
Keyloun Collection of Mola Art, designed for Neiman-
Marcus; 170, by Paul Davis, 1977, copyright © 1977 by
Paul Davis; 176, by Chuck Jones, 1978, copyright © 1978
by Warner Brothers, Inc.; 180, by Kip Lott, 1979, cover
illustration *After Magritte* by Kip Lott; 186, by B. Kliban,
1980, copyright © by B. Kliban, 1980; 192, by Tom Wood,
1981, copyright © 1981 by Walt Disney.

C·O·N·T·E·N·T·S

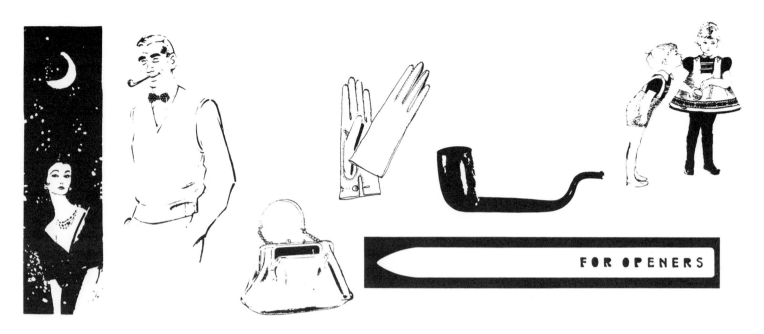

FOR OPENERS

To my assistant, Alice Snavely, I express my deep appreciation for her untiring efforts, which made this book possible. To Dr. Carol Evans, archivist at Neiman-Marcus, my thanks for her painstaking research. To Debbie Borum, Wanda Lampier, and Hortense Spitz Shair, my gratitude for their many efforts.

The contributions of material came from many individuals, now or formerly associated with Neiman-Marcus. To all of them I am deeply indebted. I single out Tom Barnett, Ron Foppen, John Giesecke, Kay Kerr, John Himelfarb, Roger Horchow, Johnny Lemmon, the late C. C. Rowland, and Don Shipman in particular, but not in exclusion of a hundred others who helped stir my own recollections.

**75th Anniversary
1907 - 1982**

Neiman-Marcus

STANLEY MARCUS

Chairman Emeritus
Neiman-Marcus

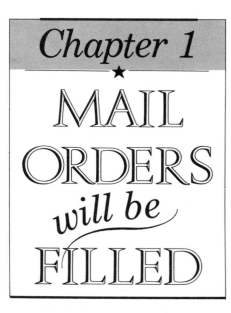

Chapter 1
★
MAIL ORDERS *will be* FILLED

*W*hen my father, Herbert Marcus, wrote the early Neiman-Marcus advertisements, he used every convincing reason he could to bring customers into his new store. He extolled the quality and beauty of the merchandise and the superiority of the service in an attempt to establish the fashion authority of his new emporium.

From the outset, he recognized that many of the customers would be coming from neighboring towns within a hundred-mile radius. He was gratified when fashion-hungry ladies showed up from Arkansas, Oklahoma, and Louisiana, as well as from the remote corners of Texas, in response to his initial Dallas Morning News advertisement, in which he stated: "As well as the Store of Fashion we will be known as the Store of Quality and Superior Values. We shall be hypercritical in our selections. Only the finest productions of the best garment makers are good enough for us. Every apparel article shown will bear evidence in its touches of exclusiveness, in its chic and grace and splendid finish, to the most skillful and thorough workmanship."

No mention was made in the first advertisement of a mail order service, but the demands of out-of-town customers must have been felt very quickly, as evidenced by an ad on February 2, 1908, a bare five months after the opening, in which it was stated, "Will fill all mail orders with the utmost care. Garments will be fitted on models in sizes ordered before sending, assuring satisfactory garments."

I doubt if my father realized that he was laying the foundation for a large and dynamic mail order business that would eventually produce catalogues with a circulation of a million and a half. As a good merchant, he was simply interested in meeting the demands of his customers, whether they lived in Dallas or out of town. Sending expensive clothes through the mails was time-consuming and risky. It was too easy for a woman to fail to understand the new fashions without the benefit of an attendant salesperson or too tempting for a customer to show the gowns to her dressmaker to copy. In many

The value of convention traffic was noted in an advertisement on May 5, 1912: "Reduced rates on all railroads during Retail Merchants' Association convention from all Texas points"; and again on October 5, 1913: "Out-of-town patrons are a great asset to this business. . . . Linked by great systems of interurban and steam railroads, Dallas has been for years the great retail shopping center of Texas. . . ."

instances, as I learned later, he would send his best saleswoman and a fitter with a trunkful of clothes by train to Camden, Arkansas, or Rushton, Louisiana, or to Houston, Texas, to sell and fit the clothes on the spot. It was an expensive procedure, but one that firmly entrenched Neiman-Marcus as a reliable and painstaking source of supply for many of the wealthiest women of the Southwest.

Dallas women supported Neiman-Marcus from the outset, but in 1907 Dallas had a total population of some eighty-four thousand inhabitants. There are no demographics available for that time, but it is a reasonable assumption that the number of affluent and fashion-conscious women in the area was limited. Thus it was natural for the new store to reach out to attract more customers in the region by any and all methods. From February 2, 1908, on, almost every advertisement made reference to "out-of-town patrons" and to "visitors, not only of our own state, but from Eastern cities."

In January 1915, with World War I in progress and the price of cotton down to ten cents a pound, the store promoted its mail order service with great energy. On January 3 of that year, a full-page ad announced, "We will take especial care to fill mail orders promptly during this sale. On account of the limited number of garments we advise that first, second, and third choices be specified. This will assist us in sending you something suitable in the event that your first choice is sold before order is received." At the bottom of the page was an additional reminder: "Take advantage of our telephone and mail service. Prompt delivery." In February, the ad stated, "Mail orders are being received in constantly increasing volume. Invariably they are handled to the customers' utmost satisfaction." And again in August, "Shopping by mail is just as satisfactory as when done in person. We make it as near like a personal transaction as possible. Individual tastes are considered and close attention is given to every order."

The grammar might have been improved in several instances, but the persuasiveness of the copy could hardly be criticized. Undoubtedly, the store was feeling the pinch of the war on the local economy. Since Dallas was an important inland cotton market, the government prohibitions against selling and shipping cotton overseas had an adverse effect on the store's most important customers who in some way or another were involved in the cotton trade—hence, the concerted drive to attract business from other cities covered by the regional circulation of the Dallas Morning News.

Once established, the mail order arm became a permanent part of the business. A special personal shopping service was set up with instructions to fill orders with the same degree of care that the customer might exercise if she were present. I recall that in many cases my aunt, Carrie Neiman, would say, "Don't send that; Mrs. Jones doesn't like pink," or "I'll write a note so she will understand how to put it on." The rate of returned merchandise was high, but the mail order service tied the customer to the store. I remember questioning the profitability of this operation with my father, who replied, "You're probably right, but we have an obligation to these customers who need something to wear for a special occasion and can't travel to Dallas at this time. Eventually they will come to town, and we'll make up what we lose on the mail order service."

Direct mail was not in vogue for high fashion and expensive apparel, although Sears and Ward's were doing a thriving catalogue business on work clothes and hardware items. Neiman-Marcus, which was a small enterprise at that time, had neither the resources nor the experience to develop the concept of branching out into a catalogue operation. Occasional brochures and merchandise leaflets were issued; but unfortunately, little of this advertising ephemera has survived.

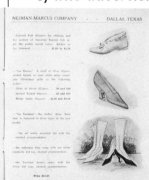

The earliest piece still extant is a small brochure, five by six inches, with six pages of Christmas gift suggestions, dated 1915. Its cover announced "The Perfect Christmas Gifts from Neiman-Marcus Co." There is no evidence of further Christmas cataloguing until 1926, when the store issued a five-by-three-inch booklet with sixteen pages of Christmas

gift suggestions. The title page carried a brief message: "This gift booklet, prepared to assist those who are looking for the unusual in gifts, is but an index to infinite gift assortments. Our special gift wrapping service has again been arranged for those who select their gifts at Neiman-Marcus. It is entirely without charge and adds greatly to the attractions of your gifts." Seventy-eight articles were sketched and described, including a number of import items, perfumes, French handbags, fur coats, and an assortment of lingerie. Discreetly, brassieres and step-in sets were described but not illustrated. In one move considered daring at the time, however, the catalogue did include a sketch and recommendation for a reptile-covered cigarette case for women! The cover of the catalogue shows the first color presentation of N–M gift-wrapped packages. This original idea, conceived by the store's advertising manager, Zula McCauley, has become one of the store's most distinctive and important services.

The catalogue just described followed my father's first trip to Europe in the summer of 1925. I had recently graduated from Harvard and as a graduation present I was invited to accompany him. My mother was unable to leave her three younger sons, so my role was to keep him company and to offset his pangs of homesickness; to learn buying techniques; and in any time that was left over to have a good time. That was the year of the Exposition Internationale des Arts Décoratifs, which so profoundly influenced the designs of architecture, furniture, textiles, and many objects of fashion. This was the birth of Art Deco.

We went to England, Germany, and France, setting up buying office connections and viewing the assortments of European goods. No buyers accompanied us, so my father had to make selections in a wide variety of product lines, ranging from perfumes to gloves, lingerie to costume jewelry. On the Atlantic crossing we had met a number of American couples, and my father leaned heavily on the buying tastes of many of the wealthy women we had just met. In those days, the finest handbags and lingerie were produced by small artisans who did not sell to the shops, but brought their wares to the hotel suites of their

customers. By following these leads, my father was able to locate goods of exceptional quality and taste. It was he who taught me to rely on the judgment of the discriminating, wealthy American woman.

He observed the glove lengths these women preferred, the size handkerchiefs they bought for their personal use, the cut steel buckles they put on their shoes. One of our friends had purchased a Spanish shawl and wore it to dinner at Ciro's, the most chic café in Paris, creating a sensation. He followed her lead and bought a large selection which was introduced to America through the 1926 catalogue. After this fashion had ebbed many women used the shawls to drape over their grand pianos.

Although the catalogue was modest in size and restrained in format, it established a philosophy that was to become the basis of future catalogues. It showed unusual articles, many of which were imported, in a wide variety of prices, with keen emphasis on selectivity and taste. It was the first example of Neiman-Marcus's move to establish itself as a pre-eminent gift store and its desire to enhance its gifts with beautiful and excitingly gift-wrapped packages. Fifty-six years later the same objectives still prevail—only the gift wraps are no longer free!

*I*n the course of writing this book, I reviewed every surviving Neiman-Marcus catalogue from 1926 through 1981. It's a tremendously interesting history of transition: a transition from silk to Qiana, from wool to Orlon, from the practical to the fantastical, from peace to war and back to peace, from prosperity to recession, from an emphasis on negligees for the boudoir to the relaxed lifestyle of the patio, and from spectator clothes to the active jogging outfits of today. In the pages of the catalogue you see the effects of inflation, the changes in the economy, and the technological advances that brought forth all of the electronic wonders of the day. In 1942, the catalogue specified that no orders for monogrammed handkerchiefs would be accepted after December 15. Today, it is rare to find handkerchiefs in the catalogue at all, for since the advent of Kleenex tissues, handkerchiefs have declined in usage. Currently, articles to be monogrammed oftentimes require from three to six weeks' time for delivery.

It is interesting to observe the ingenuity of the Neiman-Marcus buyers and manufacturers when challenged to develop specialized items exclusively for Neiman-Marcus. Over the years the increasing rigidity of mass production has made these achievements less frequent. Vendor financial participation began to show up actively around 1958, although we had traditionally used the names of perfumers and hosiery makers to finance the high costs of production of the earlier catalogue. Today, virtually every article in the catalogue has a supplier's name buried somewhere in the copy to indicate his contribution for space representation. This isn't at all bad, because the manufacturer is getting his money's worth for advertising his name in a distinguished publication; but it does raise the unhappy question as to how many worthwhile objects don't get into the catalogue because of a lack of participative money from the maker.

After having made this review of many years of Neiman-Marcus advertising in newspapers, magazines, and catalogues, I couldn't help feeling that it had stood the test of time extremely well and reflected quite consistently the Neiman-Marcus standards of refinement and good taste, one of the store's basic objectives from the very beginning. The catalogues' designers avoided the influences of the Playboy era and usually succeeded in depicting lingerie with circumspection and dignity, not yielding to the easy temptation to make the depiction flamboyant, sexy, and prurient.

Many of the results of technology in synthetic textiles, electronics, and scientific breeding of furs made their initial public appearances in the pages of the N–M Christmas catalogues.

There were relatively few lapses of taste considering the time span covered. We showed a frilled evening shirt in bright yellow, which I am glad to say our customers rejected completely. In the 1977 catalogue, to advertise a set of printed sheets we showed a man in bed who looked little like the typical Neiman-Marcus customer to whom we were appealing. Again in 1977, we succeeded in taking

*T*he path of inflation can be charted by the charges on gift wraps, which in 1962 were gratis on purchases of $100 and over; whereas in 1980, the minimum was $200 gratis and $3 per package below that figure. One constant gift article over a period of twenty years is the man's pocket knife with several blades and a folding pair of scissors. This was introduced in the catalogue of 1952 at $2.50. It held its price for six or seven years, and then it started to advance to $3.95 in 1959; to $7.50 in 1973; and finally, in 1981, it reached $17.

two perfectly beautiful girls dressed in lingerie and making them look like ladies out of an old photograph from a bordello. In 1980, there was a pair of sachet packages featured that were so corny that they looked like they might have come from the competition of a state fair handicraft show. However, these are minor blemishes on an otherwise beautiful face, and they probably won't be long remembered. As a perfectionist, I look through every catalogue with a searching eye; I am still living for the day when I will see a perfect Neiman-Marcus catalogue with no mistakes of taste, judgment, or production of any kind. I doubt if I shall live that long.

In our early days of cataloguing, we made a special attempt to get the catalogue in the hands of the dozen or so wealthiest citizens of small towns, not only in the Dallas market area, but up and down the Mississippi Valley. We felt that these people would be more responsive to our catalogues than well-to-do prospects in major cities of the East and West Coasts. For the first five years or so, these accounts proved to be our most responsive ones; but later, as the catalogue became popular throughout the country, we were interested to find that large numbers of our mail orders came not from isolated rural communities, but from big cities such as Chicago, New York, Philadelphia, and Boston.

When the subject of the Neiman-Marcus Christmas catalogue comes up, invariably the question is asked, "What is the most expensive thing Neiman-Marcus has ever sold from the catalogue?" The next question is, "Do people really buy any of the exotic objects advertised?" The answer to the first question is that the single largest sale was a chamois bag of loose assorted sizes of diamonds for $197,850 in 1973.

The answer to the second is that normally we will sell at least one, or maybe a half, of the esoteric gifts of the year. Sometimes we will sell many more, as in the case of the Chinese junks we offered in 1962, when to our amazement we received orders for eight junks. When we put such items in the catalogue, we have to be prepared to sell at least one, with some reserve backup in case we get a surprisingly large number of orders. Unfortunately, there is no forecasting technique to ascertain the type of *response that we will receive. The main purpose of these unusual gift suggestions is not the sales, though we are glad to get them, but the publicity that ensues from their appearance in the catalogue. Each year's publication, of course, succeeds in adding to the legend, as more and more people become attracted to the catalogue, partly from curiosity, and partly from the desire to buy from Neiman-Marcus.*

Fulfillment is the name given to the process of servicing customers' mail orders. Obviously, the speed with which they are filled and the percentage of cancellations are the prime indicators of the efficiency of any mail order operation. The faster an order is delivered, the greater is customer satisfaction, for the mail order buyer is just like the store buyer in wanting delivery after purchase as fast as possible. Any catalogue item carrying a notation of "allow four to ten weeks for delivery" is a sure indication that the cataloguer is not carrying the item in stock but is relying on the supplier to provide the inventory.

No cataloguer is immune from cancellations, for the variables ranging from manufacturer failure to unforeseeable demand make it impossible to maintain a perfect record. If a cataloguer were able to fill every order for every size up to the day before Christmas, he would necessarily be overstocked after the season was over. Consequently, he must plan for a small percentage of cancellations if he is to remain solvent. A cancellation ratio ranging between 5 and 8 percent is considered to be an indicator of efficient operation.

The nature of the N–M catalogue makes it a tempting target for would-be big shots who attempt to impress their girl friends or party companions by calling long distance to order some of the more fabulous gift items. Sometimes the orders stick; sometimes they are canceled during the early hours of the following day. Many Neiman-Marcus customers have such large buying power that we are forced to treat each order seriously and with the respect that it is a bona fide *request, after having subjected it to the normal credit clearance. Pranksters enjoy pulling our leg by ordering a gift to be sent to some remote corner of the world or by making a call from*

*O*n December 15, 1969, the director of mail order was advised that London was calling. The man on the other end had a foreign accent and identified himself as the secretary of the sheik of an important Middle Eastern country. He was inquiring on behalf of the sheik whether we could deliver twenty-four baby elephants, of the size featured on the "Growth Gifts" page, by New Year's Day for a party that the sheik was giving at an unspecified valley located between two mountains. The secretary was meticulous about the details, and the call lasted for over half an hour.

He explained that there would be a giant-sized chess field marked off in the valley and that each elephant would be decorated to represent the specific chess pieces. Each of ▷▷

◁the animals would be mounted by men with walkie-talkies so that they could respond to the movement commands from the players located on the neighboring mountains.

The mail order director thought this might be a gag, but we handled it with complete seriousness, quoting prices and supplying information about transportation and delivery dates. He asked for banking references, which were furnished by the caller. A check with the London bank confirmed the fact that this was a prank. We had no idea who had gone to all the trouble and expense of the call until the next day, when we learned that the whole episode had been conceived and executed by a well-known disc jockey in Los Angeles.

The mail order director wanted to retaliate by renting an elephant in Los Angeles to be delivered to the deejay at the radio station with the information that the other twenty-three were on the way, together with a bill.

The idea was tempting, but I vetoed it in the belief that any further publicizing of the joke would only encourage others to try to outdo it.

overseas for one of the exotic "His and Her" gifts.

No customer who receives a cancellation is satisfied with either a statistical answer or any explanation for failure to fill the order. "You have ruined my Christmas," is the complaint most commonly heard when we have to send out a notice that the supply is exhausted. We even telephone customers by long distance to explain the situation and offer to make substitutions; or we will check stocks in all of our stores to see if, by chance, the needed size and color is available to fill the order. By a quirk of fate, we had an item in the 1979 book that had a component made in Iran, and when the hostage crisis occurred in that country all shipments were cut off. We had no choice but to cancel the several thousand orders we were holding.

The use of the 800 toll-free telephone number has helped to maintain better communications with the hundreds of thousands of customers who order from the catalogue. Occasionally, one of our out-of-town patrons will call the toll-free number to ask our order taker to look up a street address or telephone number of a friend in the Dallas area. One lady even used the number to ask us to make appointments with her favorite hairdresser.

Some of our order takers establish a very friendly rapport with customers over the years, getting to know the names of the children and other members of the family for whom gifts are being ordered. They bend over backwards in their efforts to satisfy a request, even to the point of buying an article at retail in another store when we have exhausted our supply. Not infrequently, customers will call after Christmas to inquire if a particular item proved to be a good seller.

We have had anguished calls from customers who have returned jewel boxes in which they placed thousands of dollars of jewelry or even false teeth. We've had to run down these returned packages in the midst of a busy Christmas season to retrieve the customers' property. Thus far, we have been successful.

At one time we had a star mail order customer who had never visited the store but who regularly ordered from $20,000 to $30,000 worth of gifts from the Christmas catalogue. She never telephoned; she didn't even use the

*O*ne woman, who was divorced and had remarried, didn't want her first husband to know her address. She had ordered some Christmas presents to be sent to her children, who were living with the father. When she became aware that the gifts carried the name and address of the sender, she called us in a panic and requested that the sales slip carrying that information be removed from the packages. A work force of twenty people went through thirty-five thousand gift-wrapped boxes to locate her purchases. We finally found them in a United Parcel Service delivery van and pulled out the revealing information. She was convinced that if her ex-husband learned her current address, he would kill her. So we may have saved a life.

mail order form; she simply annotated the catalogue with the name and address of the recipient alongside each of the articles she was ordering. Her handwriting was not the easiest to decipher, so we assigned one of our most experienced staff members to handle her annual orders personally, even to supervise the gift wrappings and the placement of her purchases in the mail.

We currently have a customer who orders gifts worth $10,000 to $15,000 from each catalogue, which he pays for in cash but then returns 90 percent for credit. We've been hoping his record will improve so that we won't have to inform him that we can't afford the luxury of his business.

There's always excitement in the mail order receiving room when orders come in from famous people like the Rockefellers, heads of state, television personalities, astronauts, sports figures, and motion picture celebrities. The greatest stir comes when an order of very large size arrives from a person who is not famous at all. Frequently, those orders receive faster credit clearance than those from the big names.

Planning the Christmas catalogue is a year-round occupation; producing it, from the selection of the merchandise to the delivery of finished photography and text to the printer, is compacted into a three-month period. The actual printing on high-speed presses is a matter of a few weeks. The total effort involves a cast of close to three hundred people, some of whom work around the clock as the press deadline approaches.

Just as there are merchandise crises, so are there unforeseen problems in every catalogue production. Frequently merchandise is photographed on location thousands of miles away, in Thailand, Hawaii, Spain, or Holland, to obtain special background effects. On the final set of shots on the beach in Maui, Hawaii, one year, the camera crew was engulfed by a huge wave, ruining a whole roll of film that had taken hours to shoot. The salt water damaged the cameras, necessitating the purchase of new equipment and an extra four days of reshooting. The budget was mortally wounded.

In the early days of our catalogue business, the production of art and layouts was done by the advertising department, whose main responsibility was the creation of

When we introduced Godiva chocolates we had no previous experience in shipping fine chocolates through the mail. To assure freshness of the candy on receipt, we purposely scheduled late delivery from the manufacturer, which unfortunately resulted in delayed shipments to our customers.

Leland Hayward, the producer of such stage hits as *South Pacific*, ordered three boxes; when they had failed to arrive by December 10, he dispatched hot letters of complaint to the candy department, the director of mail order, and me. Each of the recipients reacted independently, sending a letter of apology and an air-mailed replacement order. By the time he received them the original order also arrived, giving him a total of twelve boxes. This led to an acerbic note from Mr. Hayward to the effect that "obviously the left hand of Neiman-Marcus doesn't know what the right hand is doing." He was correct.

the daily newspaper advertising. We couldn't afford the luxury of a separate staff to produce one catalogue a year. Later, when the mail order business skyrocketed in volume, we did install a self-sustaining department with its own art director, artists, production manager, and copywriters. Many talented people, who made great contributions to the distinctiveness of Neiman-Marcus mail order, have come through the two departments. One outstanding person was a young artist, Joe Hong, who had been engaged to do gift-wrap designs. One year, when the advertising art director got far behind in his newspaper work, he suggested that we turn over the catalogue design to Hong.

We had completed the laborious task of merchandise selection, and we gave Joe ten days to come up with his layouts. At the appointed time, there was no sign of Joe. On inquiry we learned that he had gone to the city dump to try to retrieve his design and catalogue cover, both of which he had completed in the wee hours of the morning. Somehow they had been knocked off his drawing board onto the floor, where they had been swept out with the morning trash. He went through the city dump heaps without success. There was nothing else to do but to start over. Another appointment was set up for ten days later.

Again, Joe failed to show up. This time we located him sound asleep at home. He had worked until 3:00 A.M. and had not heard his alarm. The work was superb, and I complimented him warmly. After he left I asked the production manager, Johnny Lemmon, to stay behind. "Johnny," I said, "I saw the expression on your face when Joe finally showed up. There was no doubt in your mind that I was going to fire him on the spot, right?" "Right," he replied. "You are new in your job," I told him, "and there is something you're going to have to learn that I learned a long time ago in working with creative people. If they did everything we expected them to do on schedule, there would be no reason for you or me to be around. Someone has to keep them organized. If you get the superlative work you want, you have to put up with a lot of idiosyncrasies." I think that's why we attract and keep the many talented people who come to work in our advertising departments.

*I*n the late sixties, we received an order from a Greek shipping magnate for a giant-sized stuffed panda, measuring about five feet in height. The order came three days before Christmas with instructions to ship it by air. We had it in stock, but there was no way to get any shipper to guarantee its delivery by Christmas Day. We called the purchaser and explained the situation. He said that he had to have it and that we should buy two first-class plane seats so that the panda could ride as a passenger. The chaperone, he assured us, would have a week's holiday in Greece with his compliments. There was only one restriction: we should not use his rival's carrier, Olympic Airlines! We did not ask why. The panda arrived on time, and fortunately we avoided any publicity on this extraordinary delivery.

If we ever charged the catalogue project with the time spent by all of the people engaged with its production and the mental anguish involved, I doubt if we could afford to publish it. It's better that we don't know its full cost.

I have had the opportunity to witness the growth of an idea into a big and profitable business. That is a reward in itself, for too many times individuals don't live long enough to see an idea mature. I've witnessed the establishment of many firms whose products contributed to the uniqueness of the N–M catalogue, and in turn, I've observed the development of their own success as suppliers. I saw my brother Eddie's tremendous contribution to this important aspect of the Neiman-Marcus business. I have relished the worldwide publicity that the catalogue produces for the company, making Neiman-Marcus possibly the best-known name in high quality retailing. The fame of the catalogue preceded the establishment of Neiman-Marcus stores across the country and, understandably, made it easier to put down roots in faraway places. I have enjoyed the opportunity to serve customers all over the world and to help enrich their celebrations of Christmas.

The N–M catalogue has been a perpetual source of interest for radio and TV shows, not only at Christmas but throughout the year. Regardless of when I have been a guest on an interview show, the one certain question to be asked is, "Why do you put those exotic articles in your Christmas catalogue?" To which I reply, "To get someone like you to ask me that question on TV."

For several years the "Today Show" has invited Neiman-Marcus to make its first public unveiling of the feature gifts of the year on its program. Its widespread audience assures maximum coverage for this momentous disclosure. In 1981, my son Richard Marcus appeared on it along with Jerome Hamlin, the inventor of the ComRo I, the "His and Her" robot. The robot was left in the studio overnight in good working condition. The next morning, a few minutes before show time, it was discovered that the battery in this masterpiece of human ingenuity had run down. Presumably someone on the night crew had been playing with it and had failed to turn off the switch.

*O*f the hundreds of letters of appreciation, none seems to capsule the complete experiences of Christmas shopping with Neiman-Marcus as does this one from Michigan:

... I was so smitten with it, they insisted that I take it back home ... that was the beginning of my love affair with Neiman-Marcus and the start of the N-M Christmas tradition in our home.

The tradition was (is): Husband, children, and parents receive a Neiman-Marcus–wrapped gift each Christmas (the *only* gifts opened Christmas Eve). Everyone knew that the N-M package had to be cautiously opened, because once their gift was removed, the box would be carefully re-wrapped to be used for on-going Christmas decor.

As the years passed, we become over-packaged, so we reverted to the ''hanging'' wall-of-tribute to Neiman-Marcus Christmas.

In the meanwhile, I shall keep hoping that someday, some member of my family will get the brilliant idea to order *me* a Christmas package from N-M, so I could have the pleasure of ''unassembling'' a Neiman-Marcus Christmas package as well as re-assembling it!

With kind regards,

This year she will receive a Christmas package from Neiman-Marcus. It has already been ordered, and I wish her joy in ''unassembling'' it.

The show had to go on with a feeble verbal description of this electronic marvel instead of an actual demonstration. The experience merely went to prove that as long as we have humans we shall continue to have computer failures.

*O*ur method of putting the catalogue together was built around a selection committee, which sat in judgment as sixty-five buyers brought in their gift candidates for acceptance or rejection. Christmas catalogue selection became a very tedious business, particularly since these meetings took place in June, when the temperature was 105 degrees outside. As Warren Leslie, an early sales promotion manager, reported in his Wales newspaper column, we even resorted to singing "Jingle Bells" and scattering paper snowflakes as a prelude to looking at the several thousand pieces of Christmas merchandise that would be paraded before us.

Sometimes the buyers had finished merchandise; other times they brought in rough samples, sketches, or photographs, gathered from their domestic and foreign market trips. The committee, consisting of my brother Eddie and/or myself, the general merchandise manager, the art director, the production manager, and the fashion director, appraised every article from the standpoint of value, quality, fashion rightness, taste, and timeliness. We attempted to reach a consensus, but if there was none, then Eddie or I would make a final decision.

Although the committee tried to be objective, some ego assertion or ego protection was always prevalent. Many a buyer left those meetings with wounded feelings whenever a favorite brainchild was clubbed to death. Eddie and I often had sharp differences of opinion as to whether an article would sell in quantity, whether it was timely, whether it would reproduce well photographically, whether it was in good taste. Many a time we each left the meetings with ruffled feathers, irritated by the other's lack of respect for a different point of view. Usually, a good *night's sleep restored our perspectives—at least until the next disagreement.*

After all decisions were made, it became the job of the art director and his layout people to organize the several hundred items into meaningful pages that related to each other with the proper degree of harmony and continuity. It was similar to putting a jigsaw puzzle together.

Provision had to be made for substitute items, because of manufacturers' production difficulties or inability to meet our delivery requirements. These meetings ran every day from 9:00 A.M. until 5:30 P.M. for a whole week. The more sophisticated buyers jockeyed around for presentation time, realizing that the committee was in a much better mood the first thing in the morning than in the afternoon, by which time its members were groggy and much more critical. One buyer who was scheduled to show his wares at 4:30 arranged to have high tea served before his presentation. Others resorted to milder bribery by bringing up a box of chocolates or cookies to relieve the committee's hunger pangs.

Long after I ceased to have any participation in the catalogue production I learned of a trick which became known as "the art director's ruse." If he didn't like a particular article of a fragile nature, he would place it on the edge of the table in a precarious state of balance. The slightest jar to the table would cause the article to fall to the floor and break. He reported the accident, and since in most instances it was too late to get a new sample, he was then able to replace it with one of the standby selections.

The Christmas catalogue, which originally had been more or less a Christmas card used to invite customers to come to the store to start their holiday shopping, gradually became a mechanism to sell to them in their homes as well. As we gained valuable experience in the selection of merchandise that people would order by mail and the colors and sizes most likely to be in demand, our technical skills in servicing orders improved. The estimation of quantities of original purchases continued to be a gamble, for there is no proven buying formula for new and untested items. About 1945 we began to increase the size of our initial commitments and tried to persuade some of our suppliers that it was good business for them to back up our orders with similar quantities until we could develop a sales trend two weeks after the issuance of the book. We advanced the mailing date from mid-October to mid-September to give us an extra month in which to replenish stocks of articles in greatest demand.

My brother Eddie, who had a wonderful mathematical mind, developed a projection chart after the first week of catalogue distribution to give the store buyers a tentative future order forecast. He based his initial projection on the first 1,000 orders received; a week later, with additional sales results, he produced a "safe" prediction of the total number of orders that might be received during the following six weeks. Most of the time his forecast proved to be correct; but occasionally an item would reverse itself, and we would get stuck with surplus quantities. As the years progressed our skills in prognostication improved, but the element of gamble has never completely disappeared.

Very early in our cataloguing experience, Eddie foresaw the potential of electronic data processing and pressed our control division to "computerize" the mail order division. Computerization eventually proved to be a boon, but like all other installations in industry, we had our share of headaches in the early stages.

One particularly painful experience involved an offering of crystal paperweights carrying the seal of whichever of the fifty states the customer requested. We were delighted with the early sales results until one morning the mail order supervisor received a call from a puzzled customer, who reported, "I ordered a paperweight with the Wisconsin seal to be gift wrapped and sent to me. I have just received a shipment of forty-four identically wrapped packages which I suspect all contain identical paperweights. What's going on?" Our supervisor promised to investigate and report back to him.

After considerable research he found that the man was going to receive fifty-five more of them within the next

*S*ome time later we learned that computer forecasts could not foretell a drop in demand caused by overexposure of an item. This occurred at the time of the popularity of the "Star Wars" masks. On the basis of the first orders, the computer told us that we should be prepared to sell 24,782 masks, so we ordered 20,000. A week later the orders on the item dropped precipitately to two a day. We were bewildered until some non-computer entity explained that the mask was in every catalogue in distribution and in dozens of stores in every city. That experience gave us a healthy skepticism toward computer reports. For two years our warehouse shelves were filled with Darth Vader and the Chewbacca faces, until one day we discovered that kids didn't want them at any price. The whole lot was sent to the city dump.

few days. What had happened was that a faulty encodement of another order, which the computer couldn't read, had been entered into the system. This caused the computer to kick back to the Wisconsin order ninety-nine times, repeating it ninety-nine times and validating ninety-nine shipments. It was just about to order the hundredth paperweight when the error was discovered and the computer was shut off.

We explained this comedy of ninety-nine errors to our customer and asked him to return ninety-eight of them to us for credit. Needless to say, we were overstocked with Wisconsin paperweights for several years.

That first year our mailing list was put on the computer, one customer received 732 copies of the Christmas catalogue, much to his inconvenience and our embarrassment.

Chapter 2

★

The SEARCH for IDEAS

*W*hen Neiman-Marcus entered the catalogue business it had very little competition from rival books. It was the first large-scale attempt to sell medium- to high-priced high fashion merchandise through the mail, but it didn't take long for a covey of competitors to take inspiration from the Neiman-Marcus success and to publish rival books. Other stores in other cities issued publications; but few, if any, developed a basic understanding of how to mount a mail order operation independent of their retail store operations. Roger Horchow, a Neiman-Marcus alumnus, started the Kenton catalogue in 1971 and transformed it into the Horchow Collection book in 1974. He understood the business; he did it right and is deservedly successful.

Few cataloguers disclose their sales, so the only way to evaluate their success is from market gossip and the frequency of their mailings. Saks Fifth Avenue and Joseph Magnin were among the first of the specialty stores to issue competitive publications, and they were soon joined by I. Magnin and Sakowitz. Most of them designed catalogues that reflected their individual store personalities; a few attempted to emulate some of the techniques Neiman-Marcus had originated.

Roger Horchow experienced the same type of "knock-off" by imitators, but copies rarely fare as well as the originals, for the public usually perceives the difference between the two and makes its own decision. Many times my associates would become indignant when a competitor would lift an idea we had originated, but my reaction was always, "As long as we are being copied, it's a sign that we're still leading. Start to worry when competition is copying someone else." Finally, when some of the predators began to reproduce our artwork and steal whole paragraphs of copy, we decided to copyright each issue.

In the early days of our cataloguing, we were forced to send apparel to New York or Chicago to be photographed, but with the growth of both the N–M mail order business and the Horchow Collection, Dallas became a center for catalogue production. Good photographers *established studios capable of doing top-quality work; models moved to Dallas because of the demand for their services; and agencies specializing in catalogue production flourished. Many of the catalogues bearing imprints from Jacksonville, Amarillo, and Atlanta are now being produced in Dallas. Our success helped to create a whole new industry for Dallas.*

The whole mail order boom puzzled many of the recipients who were now being overwhelmed by the volume of mailing pieces that stuffed their boxes. They couldn't understand how a company from Michigan, unknown to them, could have gotten hold of their names. Soon they realized that mail order lists were sold by one mailer to another. As a matter of fact, the sale of lists is still a thriving business encouraged by magazines and direct sellers. It's a practice Neiman-Marcus has never engaged in, however, because of our conviction that customers who choose to shop by mail with us are entitled to the protection of privacy. In adhering to this policy, we have forgone a large source of income.

People often ask me, "How do I get my name on your mailing list?" To which I reply, "It's very easy. I can put your name on it, but only you can keep it there by purchasing from the catalogues. The computer periodically eliminates the names of those who haven't ordered during the preceding eighteen months on the assumption that a 'no order' record indicates a lack of interest in the contents of the catalogue." The catalogue has become so expensive to produce and mail that it is mandatory to eliminate "deadwood" (non-buyers) from the mailings lists.

To discourage juveniles and other non-buyers, N–M has had to make a $3 charge to non-charge-account customers for the Christmas book. If the recipients order, their names are retained on the list; if they don't, they are dropped. Mail order customers become profitable assets in direct relationship to the frequency and continuity of their purchases. The most consistent "buyers'" names go on what is termed "a prime list." Those customers may then receive all eighteen catalogues Neiman-Marcus distributes annually, or at least those mailers containing the classification of items previously ordered.

Catalogue shopping has been stimulated by a number of factors. The lack of parking accessibility at shopping centers and downtown stores has predisposed many customers to order by catalogue from the comfort of their homes. Gasoline shortages have undoubtedly encouraged shoppers to limit trips and to order by mail. Buyers find that their catalogues actually give them fuller and more accurate information than that offered by the average store salesperson.

It would be difficult to sue a salesperson in a store for lack of knowledge of the fiber content of a shirt, but the customer does have such a recourse against the cataloguer for such failures. Consequently, all the pertinent information about the product is double-checked before the book goes to press, since a cataloguer faces disciplinary action by the Federal Trade Commission or other authorities for inaccurate descriptions. So many stores have gone over to self-service that customers have found fewer reasons for going to stores to shop, particularly when they have the alternatives offered by a variety of catalogues. Moreover, a catalogue is never impolite or rude. Direct marketing is here to stay, although the forms may change as cable television and other direct purchasing techniques become more commonly available. (This subject is discussed in detail in the final chapter.)

From the days of its founding, Neiman-Marcus has believed in the value of competition. We never wanted to be the only store on the block. When locating stores in other cities we go to those communities with other good stores, for we have always had both confidence in our ability to compete and the conviction that competition would make us better merchants.

Catalogue competition was no different. It forced us to become more creative developing our merchandise, to be more ingenious designing our books, and to select printers whose press work would be superior in quality to that of competitive mailers. To increase both the distinctiveness and beauty of our catalogues, we commissioned leading artists at home and abroad to do the covers, a practice we had started with Marcel Vertés in 1943 and 1945, Saul Steinberg in 1951, and Ludwig Bemelmans in 1955. We gave them complete freedom, as long as the subject had some reference to Christmas.

Many of our covers were reproduced on our Christmas shopping bags, and in some cases they were made into posters which were offered for sale. The use of well-known artists from the field of the fine arts unquestionably added another dimension to the prestige of the N–M catalogues and helped set them apart from the competition, just as the utilization of paintings and sculptures in our stores had made similar contributions to the mystique of Neiman-Marcus.

However handsome a catalogue's cover might be, its eventual success depends on the fashion and attractiveness of the merchandise portrayed inside. Great pressure was put on buyers to locate new merchandise and to develop articles with a freshness of appeal. Few, if any, cataloguers have the time or resources to engage in a market survey to research what the public might buy; even if they did, I doubt that the results would be meaningful, since in most cases the public doesn't know what it wants until it sees it.

The "search and create" process is delegated to the buyers who are traveling constantly to visit the numerous trade fairs in America, Europe, and the Orient. Before going off to market, there is a general review of the successes and failures of the previous book and an interpretation of buying trends indicated by the sales quantities of different articles. Items to be repeated are discussed at that time, along with recommendations for improvement of some previous best-sellers. Above all, buyers are urged to be receptive to new ideas which spring up every year. Not all buyers have the ability to foresee the sales possibilities of something that doesn't exist; some buyers are good selectors without any talent for origination. Increased competition in the mail order field and the trend toward merchandise standardization have placed a greater premium than ever on imagination and conceptual thinking.

We sent our buyers into the worldwide markets to come back with at least 10 percent exclusive articles,

I recall one incident when a buyer presented a trench coat for consideration. She proudly stated, "I found this in Belgium, and it will be exclusive with Neiman-Marcus." I inquired how it compared with a well-known, nationally distributed coat, to which she replied with some reluctance, "Well, it's not as good, but it *is* exclusive." I told her again that exclusivity was meaningless unless the item was as good or better than any competitive product.

"made for us alone," which if accepted for the catalogue would be so described in the copy. We emphasized constantly that exclusivity was significant only if the product had the concomitant virtues of quality and fashion.

There are pluses and minuses in the Neiman-Marcus mail order buying system compared to that of some of the independent cataloguers such as Horchow. Our strength lies in the fact that there are seventy-five N–M buyers and merchandise managers covering all of the markets in the world, backed up by twenty buying offices in the important world buying centers. Their assignment is to locate potential items and bring back samples for final decision by a selection committee or the mail order director. This procedure gives us the assurance of a well-balanced book containing about 400 items which have been double-checked for taste, fashion, and value.

The weakness in this procedure is that between the time of sampling and final decision, a competitive cataloguer visits some of the same markets, sees the same merchandise, and is willing and able to make an instantaneous decision. In many instances, the seller decides that the bird in hand is more valuable and closes the sale—leaving N–M out in the cold. Our recognition of this condition has led us to modify the N–M procedure to the extent that a few experienced N–M buyers have been given the authority to make on-the-spot selections. Newer buyers are required to use the telex or telephone to discuss the urgency of the case and obtain an exception to standard policy. This modified system seems to be working pretty well, but with the development of improved satellite communication we should someday be able to conduct video selection committee meetings linking up participants in several different parts of the world.

In the competition for catalogue leadership, there is a race to be first in the presentation of new products. "First" is fine and desirable if there is no concomitant sacrifice of quality. But many times the producer, in his desire to be first, has not properly tested his product or even manufactured it properly. I was never moved by a buyer's desire to be first unless I had the assurance that "first" was also "best."

*S*everal years ago, a customer had ordered ten gifts for his wife, to be individually gift wrapped and then placed inside a larger *papier-mâché* Santa Claus we had specially made for him. This was to be delivered by Christmas Eve to a ski resort in Colorado, where the couple was celebrating Christmas. On Christmas Eve morning, the husband called, irate because the package had not arrived. On investigating we learned that the Santa had been shipped via truck the week previously, but the trucking line had no idea where this particular truck was located. After four hours of frantic telephoning, we talked to the trucker's manager in Colorado, who ascertained that the shipment was on a truck *en route* to Grand Junction, where it was due to arrive in the early afternoon, too late to be transferred to another truck bound for the ski resort.

We told him of our plight and received his personal assurance ▷▷

There is nothing quite so disconcerting to a retailer as being under-priced on an article of merchandise. This is doubly so when it occurs in a catalogue, for the merchant has no chance to explain the reasons for the price variance; the customer simply orders at the lower price. Most catalogue operations have roughly the same operating costs, leading them to price goods at approximately the same markup. Occasionally, if a cataloguer is aware that an item is scheduled to go into a competitor's book, he may decide to run the same article at a lower price for embarrassment purposes only—the old loss-leader technique. This has happened to Neiman-Marcus half a dozen times in a period of forty-three years, which actually is not too bad a record. In two cases the articles had been sold to N–M on an exclusive basis. The competitive buyer, when told that the merchandise had been reserved for Neiman-Marcus, persuaded the maker to sell him single pieces for the personal use of his boss. He then proceeded to place it in his catalogue with no hope of getting additional supplies to meet orders. He duped the manufacturer, which led to the violation of our confinement agreement. Obviously, if there is price variance, it is the N–M policy to refund the difference to the customers, even to those who had already purchased and had made no complaints.

Every day's mail seems to bring new entrants to the catalogue field. There are general catalogues, specialized ones, hobby books, simple and elaborate mailings. A few of them succeed, of course, but the faster they grow, the greater is the likelihood of failure. Along with the larger circulation comes a bigger cash outlay for mailing lists, printing, and postage. Greater circulation also requires larger merchandise investments to assure prompt fulfillment of orders, greater markdowns on those items that fail to sell in anticipated quantities, and greater problems of disposing of unsold residue stocks. Even an experienced and able cataloguer like Roger Horchow found that his business had grown too fast, and he was forced to pull back on his circulation, as he relates in his amusing and informative book, An Elephant in Your Mailbox.

The fulfillment of orders with reasonable speed is one

◄that somehow, some way, he'd see that the package was delivered by that evening. After Christmas we learned how this willing Santa Claus's helper had accomplished the impossible. Since the package had missed the trucking connection to its final destination, the manager solicited the assistance of a friend who drove a postal truck and whose route took him through the village where our customer was staying. This place, however, was not an authorized stop, and only on the urgent request from the manager did he agree to carry an oversized gift to the outskirts of the town. He said if our customer would agree to meet him at a bridge three miles north of the township, he would slow down and push the package off his truck as he went by. The rendezvous took place on schedule at 10:30 p.m. Our customer retrieved the package from a snowbank in the middle of a blizzard. His wife had her Christmas gift on Christmas Eve, although a little late!

of the most taxing problems faced by catalogue operators. This requires adequate capital for inventory investment, and the courage to commit that money. Above all we need a soundly worked out system for filling the thousands of orders that pour in, and a sophisticated computer program to enable accurate forecasting of demand. With all of these in place, unhappy mix-ups and failures will still occur. Neiman-Marcus has had its full share of them, and the challenge is always how to retrieve victory from the jaws of defeat.

"Where do you find all of the unusual things that appear in your Christmas catalogues?" is a question people consistently ask me. It's not difficult for buyers to fill the pages with four hundred well-chosen articles, but to supplement these selections with never-before-seen items requires unusual effort on the part of both buyers and catalogue directors.

During my years of European shopping, I found more unusual things in retail store windows than I did in manufacturers' showrooms. The first advice I gave a new buyer prior to an initial trip abroad was to wear out shoe leather by pounding the pavement of the retail shopping areas. I theorized that most good shopkeepers put their newest and most unusual merchandise on display to attract customers. Often I found that local merchants had access to small makers who didn't know how to run an export business and whose goods were not normally shown in the traditional trade fairs.

If I saw something that interested me, I usually introduced myself to the manager and asked if he would reveal the name and address of the maker. Since I was located so far away and was not a competitor, I most often received cooperation. If I was refused, we would send someone from our office to purchase the article and run down the identity of the maker by exposing it to manufacturers of similar products. There are very few secrets in the retail and wholesale fields. Gucci is one of the few retailers who rigidly guard their sources of supply by labeling merchandise with their name alone; most other retailers permit the use of manufacturers' trademarks or handtags. Frequently, the foreign market representative accompanying me would say, "I know where that comes from, but I didn't think you would be interested in it"; to which I would reply, "I didn't either until I saw it." An attitude of constant search is an absolute must in my business.

I made it a practice to watch what certain American travelers bought as gifts to bring home, and as a result I learned a lot. When I saw one very discriminating woman purchase a dozen cut glass purse atomizers in a perfume shop, I asked her why she was buying them. She said, "Oh, they don't take up much space in my suitcase, they're not expensive, and all of my bridge club girlfriends adore them." I reported this to our perfume buyer, who said, "Those aren't new; we've had them for a couple of years." "Have we or any other store ever catalogued them?" I asked. "No," she replied, "but they've sold very well over the counter." We decided then and there to put them in the Christmas book and sold over 5,000 units at $5 each.

The customer is not always right, of course. On another occasion I followed a similar lead and made a large purchase of African-inspired wire necklaces which proved to be a complete dud. I retrieved my credibility with our costume jewelry buyer by discovering at the Flea Market in Paris an antique butterfly pin which we had copied to sell for $25. The original cost was $365; we sold 10,000 pieces of the replica for $250,000 in sales.

During our travels to faraway markets, we often stumble upon craft products that have not previously been exported to the United States. In our constant search for new gift containers, we've sometimes been able to give such craft articles completely different uses. A trip to the town of Volendam in Holland, for example, led an

*S*ome-
times incorrect shipments
are due to customer mis-
takes rather than ours. We
had offered a gift of
twelve sirloin steaks in the
catalogue, and one of our
customers ordered them
for each of his two sons.
He mistakenly wrote
twenty-four on the order
blank instead of two and,
as a result, each of his
sons received 288 steaks.
They had no storage for
that many steaks, nor did
our customer wish to make
such a large expenditure
on his sons' Christmas
gifts. We told him to return
the surplus steaks to us for
credit, since we realized
he had made an honest
error.

*imaginative buyer to purchase a huge quantity of Dutch
wooden shoes, which she then packed with men's
toiletries. The item sold so well that she and her
assistants had to spend the week preceding Christmas
stuffing wooden shoes. While the toiletry items were good,
they would not have sold in such quantities had they been
traditionally packaged. Certainly there was no demand in
the U.S. for Dutch wooden shoes as such, but the
combination of the two made a market for both.*

*In India we came across some attractive lightweight
stools made of rush. They weren't of fine enough quality to
offer for sale as stools, but when turned upside down they
became excellent containers for gourmet foods. Since they
were bulky, freight charges would have been prohibitive;
our agent solved that problem by packing all of our
purchases of Indian brassware in them, reducing the
shipping costs of the stools considerably.*

*In this constant search for novel ideas, success is
never guaranteed. Putting together the annual N–M
Christmas catalogue is, in a way, much like producing a
new play on Broadway. Despite the collective judgments
of the knowledgeable professionals involved, the final
decision is made by the audience—and the critics. In
cataloguing, though, we don't have to await the critics'
judgment; the customers make the decision, and the
number of orders received tells us immediately whether
the item is good or bad.*

*Sometimes the quantity of orders falls short of
anticipation, leaving sizable stock remainders. In other
cases, few if any orders show up. Fortunately, we don't
have many instances of the latter. One Christmas, though,
we catalogued what we thought was an attractive
thermometer in a sterling silver case, ordering 10,000
units as coverage. After Christmas we inventoried 10,015.
We could only presume that they had bred. "Turkey" is
the name given to catalogue failures in the mail order
world, and "a turkey in your mailbox" is the descriptive
label applied to the few orders that trickle in for such
duds.*

*Once a new buyer in N–M's epicure department found
a clear sugar crystal Christmas tree ornament. He became*

One of the penalties for having a reputation for being able to meet any request is that we receive large numbers of difficult-to-fill orders. Once our mail order telephone service had a call from Hawaii from a man who wanted to order something that was not in the catalogue. He prefaced his request by saying, "I know this is unreasonable, but I figured if anyone in the country could help me out, it would be Neiman-Marcus." He wanted a Shetland pony for his grandson in Oregon. It had to be a gelding. Finding the pony was not difficult, but we were unable to locate a shipper. After research, we recommended that the pony be sent by air freight. When we called him back to inform him of the total cost, he approved it and said, "I knew Neiman-Marcus wouldn't let me down." As an added measure of his appreciation, he then gave us an order for thirty-seven gift bonds!

so excited about its beauty that he gave the vendor an order for 60,000 units. They were handmade in a small French village in the Pyrenees Mountains. He didn't even have to ask for exclusivity because the quantity required the productive efforts of half the village's inhabitants for a period of four and a half months. The buyer was positive he had a fantastic item, but the public thought otherwise. Only 18,000 orders arrived, making it the flop of the season. Yet the buyer received no criticism from his superiors, for we know the selection process of cataloguing of Neiman-Marcus must always be somewhat speculative. You win some; you lose some.

International press coverage of the N–M catalogue has inspired a flood of merchandise suggestions and proposals for the "His and Her" gifts. Housewives who were skilled in crocheting booties and bed coverlets, inventors who had patents on articles yet to be produced, and inheritors who were in possession of rare family heirlooms flooded us with proposals.

Merchandise offerings come to us from a variety of sources: by mail, by telephone, by personal presentation, and by tips from interested friends. In 1975 we learned of the existence of a herd of buffaloes through a letter from the breeder, who sent photographs. This suggestion came to us too late for use that year but was picked up for the following year's catalogue in 1976. Few contributors recognize that catalogue preparation starts almost immediately after Christmas for the next Christmas, and that by the first of July the book is being put to bed. Consequently, ideas that arrive after April 1 must be held over for the next year.

The dinosaur hunt which was used in 1975 came to us in the mail, as did the "His and Her" ostriches of 1980. The "His and Her" robot used in 1981 was the result of a letter from an American friend in Greece who knew the inventor. I advised him that I was retired from the store but would forward his proposal to the mail order director for consideration; all of which is by way of proof that mail is carefully read by N–M mail order executives and is an important source of inspiration.

Every proposal is given serious review with the hope

that we will make a sensational discovery. Only rarely does that occur. Most of the recommendations turn out to be repeat appearances of items rejected previously for failure to meet standards of quality and taste.

It was always difficult to explain why "His and Her" deluxe campers lacked the appeal of Chinese junks or why "His and Her" French poodles would not produce the same news reaction as "His and Her" camels. Every year, "His and Her" islands in the Pacific or Caribbean, "His and Her" castles in the Rhineland, and "His and Her" hand-painted portraits are invariably among the proposals.

If my arrival in a foreign city was publicized in advance, I would be inundated by a flood of bizarre conceptions of things that "would be just right for the Neiman-Marcus catalogue." Actually, "His and Her" mummy cases were offered to me on the phone by a man who had learned that I was in London. That proved to be such a smash'hit that it gave me renewed incentive to look and listen to anything and anybody.

Perhaps the most unusual offering ever made to me occurred in Paris when a man phoned for an appointment to acquaint me with "a most remarkable opportunity." I tried to get some inkling of what it was all about; if he were presenting a piano or a bulldozer, I could explain that these items, however valuable, were outside our areas of merchandising; but he wouldn't give me the slightest hint, and insisted that a personal meeting was necessary.

The following morning he arrived, accompanied by a beautiful blonde young woman and carrying a large wooden box, which he placed with great care on the center of my desk. By the way he was staging the presentation it was obvious that he was intent on riveting my attention.

"Mr. Marcus," he began, "you are the first person aside from my associates who will have seen what I am about to show. I have awaited your arrival, for I know that you are the only dealer in the United States who has both the vision and the ability to sell it. I am about to reveal to you the work of a young genius I discovered, who has done something never before achieved." With that

Neiman-Marcus Christmas mailings go to every city in the world. We even reach some penal institutions, as we discovered when we received a letter about the non-delivery of a catalogue. A complaint from an inmate prompted this answer, which was published in a Monday morning column which we formerly ran in the *Dallas Morning News.*

Neiman-Marcus

DALLAS, TEXAS 75201
December 19, 1970

MR. # 258610
STATE PRISON, U.S.A.

DEAR SHUT-IN:

Our Christmas catalogue is distributed to all fifty states and to virtually every country in the world. Your copy was sent to your home charge address, and was eventually forwarded to your current address. This is the first time, to my knowledge, that it has penetrated prison walls.

Your Christmas card order was dispatched within a month of the receipt of your order, but because our Mail Order Department was not familiar with prison regulations they did not follow the proper procedure in shipping the package to you.

They were readdressed properly, we hope, and I trust that the personally imprinted cards reached you in time for distribution to reach their European and Oriental destinations before Christmas.

We were unaware of your "unfortunate change of address," but even under such circumstances we do wish you a Merry Christmas and a Happier New Year.

Sincerely,

Stanley Marcus

Stanley Marcus

SM:GS

PHONE: RIVERSIDE 1-6911
CABLE: NEMARCO • DALLAS
From the President's letter files.

peroration, as if on signal, the blonde young woman removed the wooden case, revealing a black velvet box twenty inches square.

"The artist could have made this object in any metal, but he chose twenty-two karat gold as the proper medium." He then lifted the top of the box, and there on a six-inch base rested an object enshrouded by a piece of white satin. "Only twelve casts have been made, and they have all been reserved for your store, which will have no difficulty in selling them to your wealthy Texas customers at $100,000 each. One final word: the identity of the model must remain anonymous." His assistant unveiled the object with a dramatic snap of her wrists. Revealed was a life-size gold sculpture of a part of the female anatomy.

For a moment I thought I had been set up for a gag by Art Buchwald or another of my Paris-domiciled friends, but one look at my visitor convinced me that he was deadly serious. I thanked him for the privilege he had given me and the compliment he had paid us, but added, "You, like so many Europeans, are under a false illusion about the purchasing habits of rich Texans. Some of them are art collectors; but most of them spend their money investing in cattle, ranches, jewels, and more oil wells. Above all, they are not people to whom anything that is expensive can be sold. Furthermore, Texas has a very conservative citizenship, and the public exhibition of this piece would offend a large number of people. Our store could never place itself in that position."

"Oh, in that case you should show it privately behind closed doors."

"No, Neiman-Marcus conducts its business in the open," I replied.

He was crestfallen. I could see that he was mystified by my decision; I had destroyed his whole concept of Texas and Texans. I never saw or heard from him again, or of his twenty-two-karat-gold sculpture. As things have turned out, though, with the dramatic change in the value of gold, a $100,000 sculpture investment would now be worth a lot more.

This experience did not deter me from listening to many proposals over the years. One led to the acquisition

*O*ur computerized operations are constantly improving, but there is still ample margin for human error. Considering the huge number of orders handled every Christmas, it's not surprising that our staff occasionally mixes up an order. Here is a letter that recounts the full details of one embarrassing incident:

Dear Sir:
I was invited to a party hosted by a couple of "Gay" people in San Jose, one of whom happened to be Jewish. Imagine my delight in early November, when looking ▷▷

of the entire stock of a distinguished antique dealer; another to the purchase of a collection of museum-quality, seventeenth-century, lace-trimmed handkerchiefs; and another to a privately owned group of Chinese court robes, which we bought and promptly sold to a man who donated them to the Metropolitan Museum. One good buy can compensate for the time spent considering a hundred bad proposals.

It is a source of gratification that in our search for novel products, we have helped encourage numerous small suppliers and have actually been responsible for keeping many of them in business. On occasion our orders have been too large for a new firm to handle, in which case we've taught the manufacturers how to subcontract; in others we have advanced payments prior to the shipment of purchases to help the firm finance work-in-progress. We've even supplied designs to artisans needing that kind of assistance.

This kind of relationship has been mutually beneficial, for it has enabled us to get exclusive merchandise and at the same time assist ambitious young manufacturers in getting started. There are scores of suppliers around the world who will bear testimony to the helpful hand Neiman-Marcus and its buyers extended them.

In the 1964 catalogue we had a run on a set of fruit-decorated coffee mugs that generated more volume than the English maker could produce. Four years later we gave the idea to two young men who had recently started in business, with the suggestion that they try to find a source that could supply the necessary quantities. They changed the fruit designs, took it to Japan, and came back with an improved item, which drew over 5,000 orders. It also firmly established the new firm, Fitz and Floyd, which became the most successful importers of Japanese porcelain ware.

through your catalog, I saw a Bagel Butler. The perfect gift for the party—one that would not be duplicated by anyone else. When the gift arrived, I was so excited. It was wrapped in Christmas wrapping and was beautiful. Since it was wrapped so beautifully, I couldn't look at it; and since it came from Neiman-Marcus, I assumed that there was no need. Not being Jewish, and being one of the straight people at the party, it was very important for me to make a good impression. Imagine my horror when the gift was opened in front of the other guests and found to contain (of all things) a FRUITCAKE, instead of a Bagel Butler. Imagine my embarrassment at trying to explain that the great Neiman-Marcus Co. had made the error. The only thing that saved my life was the fact that the sales check (stating—1 Bagel Butler) was inside the box. Please send the Bagel Butler post haste, so that I can mend the break in the friendship. Also, imagine the consternation of the person expecting to receive a fruitcake. I hope that person was Jewish and would know a Bagel Butler when he saw one. . . .

Anxiously waiting your reply, I remain

Very truly yours,

A week prior to the day that 1,500,000 copies of the Neiman-Marcus Christmas catalogue are dumped into six different post offices around the country, some 2,000 special copies, appropriately gift wrapped, are sent by special delivery or hand carried to newspapers, wire service offices, columnists, and radio and TV stations to give the media the opportunity to review the book before it becomes public. In some instances, the catalogue has been personally delivered to an important columnist or commentator by Tom Alexander, executive vice-president in charge of marketing and sales promotion, to ensure that our catalogue is not buried under twenty-five other catalogues arriving about the same time.

The media are hungry for a lively lead on the forthcoming Christmas season, and the Neiman-Marcus Christmas catalogue has proved itself to be a good starting point. Since every writer and commentator knows that competitive writers and commentators are going to use the book to start their Christmas seasons, no one wants to be left behind; no one wants to take the chance that the competition will scoop them on an earth-shaking gift idea. The success of previous years' catalogues from Neiman-Marcus helps continue the legend. Each year adds another layer of legend-building material, and media coverage increases accordingly.

Whereas the catalogue automatically received recognition in its early days from the Dallas press and perhaps the national TV networks, it now receives coverage from all of the domestic wire services, a large number of individual columnists scattered over the nation, and from international publications such as London's Punch *magazine,* Paris Match, *the British Broadcasting Corporation, Radio Luxemburg, the Singapore* Sunday Times, *the* Zurich Zeitung, *and the Bermuda* Royal Gazette. *On average, there are forty-two radio interviews with some store executive about the catalogue, three TV appearances, seven lead editorials, and five nationally syndicated articles from the wire services. No serious attempts have been made to calculate the number of lines of free publicity or the minutes of radio and TV time; but if such a figure could be put together, its value would be astronomic.*

Publicity in itself doesn't mean much, since any individual or company can obtain publicity by a sensational antisocial act. But the publicity that has resulted from coverage of the Neiman-Marcus catalogue has been uniformly good. Of course, there are a lot of sly digs made at some of the esoteric gifts, and some good-natured fun-poking at the store and the super-rich customers who buy its exotic gifts. Only rarely, however, has there appeared a critical commentary that could be damaging to the reputation of the company.

A satirical birthday card has been published in Canada with a drawing of a Boeing 747, around which is tied a large pink bow. Above the picture is the single word, "Extravagant." On the inside the message reads, "The age of extravagance ended on April 23rd, 1971. That was the day Neiman-Marcus decided to offer brushed aluminum bedpans as the featured gift in their catalogue."

The kinds of publicity discussed above are valuable only as they reflect the fact that the catalogue has captured the public imagination, that it's newsworthy, and that it's interesting. If the catalogue had none of these qualities, not a single line would have been written.

The circulation growth of the catalogue is testimony to the demand created for it. The catalogue circulation has moved progressively from 50,000 in 1948, to 100,000 in 1956, to 829,000 in 1975, and to 1,260,000 in 1980. The 1981 print order was in excess of 1,500,000.

The final publicity commentary of 1980 came in the column "Notes on People" in the New York Times *on December 6, quoting Cleveland Amory, the author and ecologist:*

> *If you're a husband faced with the problem of a Christmas gift for the woman who has everything, forget Neiman-Marcus, he said. Adopt a Grand Canyon burro from the Grand Canyon Fund for Animals.*

Mr. Amory was the President of the Fund, and he was not being facetious. A quote like this is the end result of years of successful publicity.

Chapter 3

★

From
DEPRESSION
to
BOOM
TIMES

*S*ince N–M issued no new circular in the several years following the 1926 booklet, it is safe to assume that the opening of the enlarged and redecorated store building in 1927 and the increased cost of operations precluded the allocation of any budget for catalogue production. It must have been difficult to trace sufficient customer response to the 1926 Christmas brochure, attractive as it was, to have given the management any encouragement to establish it as an annual feature. Mail order was considered a customer service rather than a marketing tool.

Following my graduation from Harvard College and my first trip abroad, I spent one year at the Harvard Business School before I joined Neiman-Marcus in the summer of 1926. The store was undergoing a dramatic expansion, with a 100 percent enlargement of its facilities, so I decided to forgo the second year of business school in the belief that it was more important for my career growth to get established in the business at this critical time. I have never regretted that decision.

I was able to observe some of the problems in building construction and the allocation of spaces to new departments. I had the opportunity to witness the development of the final redecoration plans, with the inevitable differences of opinion between my father and his associates in regard to furniture, carpet, and color selections. That *they did not teach at the Business School.* I was a participant in the final *twenty-four-hour drive to get the store open on the scheduled day, working around the clock without sleep as workmen put on the finishing touches. The carpet-layers and painters actually completed their tasks a bare half hour before the scheduled dedication ceremonies. The excitement of a store opening can be compared only to the first night of a Broadway musical.*

My entry into the business was viewed by the staff with interest but also with some apprehension, for I had no credentials other than that I was the president's eldest son. My aunt was delighted with the prospect of teaching me fundamentals of fashion merchandising, but her husband, my Uncle Al, mistakenly considered me a threat to his authority. He had been a warm and generous uncle until the day I came into the store. From that moment on I became his target and scapegoat for everything that went wrong. I became a controversial figure between him and my father. Two years later his turbulent marriage with my aunt broke up, and my father purchased his shares in the store.

Simultaneously, other management defections occurred, leaving my father with a store doubled in size, an expanded staff payroll, an enlarged debt, and few experienced lieutenants to help administer the business. Instead of searching for assistance from the outside, he decided to shove me into the breach. It was a gamble, criticized by many at the time, but it paid off. Between intensive in-store education and dinner-table reviews of each day's activities, I soon became his recognized *deputy. The larger store with many new departments and services caught on immediately, with a volume growth from $1,000,000 in 1926 to almost $1,500,000 in 1928.*

My brother Eddie had a short-lived college career at Harvard and the University of Texas, becoming more proficient in contract bridge than in the academic curriculum. My father decided that if Eddie didn't want to study he should go to work in the store. He joined us in 1929 in time to enjoy a few months of prosperous retailing conditions before the fateful events of 1929 changed everything.

The market crash of 1929 was a dramatic prelude to the Great Depression which ensued and lasted for the next ten years. During that period of shrinking volume and profits, all efforts were directed to cost control as a matter of survival. The worst year of the Depression for Neiman-Marcus was 1932—the only year in its history in which it failed to show a profit. Gradually things began to pick up in Texas with the discovery of the great east Texas oil fields, which gave the state a huge new source of income. We dared in 1934 to enter the field of national advertising in Vogue *and* Harper's Bazaar *to attract out-of-state interest in the store and, as a result, triggered off a series of feature articles in national publications such as* Collier's *and* Life. *Suddenly we began to receive mail inquiries from all parts of the country.*

In 1936, with the celebration of the Texas Centennial in Dallas, America discovered Texas. Visitors poured in from all parts of the country to see this newly prosperous city and the

A MERRY CHRISTMAS TO YOU

NEIMAN-MARCUS

upstart store that advertised itself as "one of the five largest distributors of fine-quality merchandise in the nation." They liked what they saw, made purchases, and opened charge accounts. Overnight, our horizons had become enlarged; we realized that Neiman-Marcus could serve customers 1,500 miles away, as well as those within the traditional 100-mile radius.

The beneficent effects of the Texas Centennial and the more optimistic business climate encouraged us to publish our first large, magazine-size Christmas catalogue in 1939. This book, with a two-color and gold cover, measuring twelve by ten and a half inches, consisted of thirteen merchandise pages in which we showed 256 items. Since there were few good fashion photographers in Dallas at that time, we relied on sketches to depict articles of apparel. Our women staff artists had such difficulty drawing vigorous-looking, masculine figures that we employed an Austrian illustrator from New York, who had been doing all of Tripler's work, to do the men's sketches. We paid him $600 for six sketches, the highest price we had ever spent for artwork.

Fur coats and all of the fashion accessories, perfumes, and toys were sent to New York to be photographed there. This was our first experience in the use of photography, since our Dallas newspapers were not equipped to reproduce the fine screen photography necessary for good reproduction.

While this catalogue was aimed at our recently discovered national market, store traffic was still the primary goal. We had not *learned how to make it easy to shop by mail, a technique that took us years to acquire. No dimensions were given to the accessories or gift items; it was left to the customers to guess heights and widths. We offered articles in four or six colors, thus vastly complicating the problem of filling mail orders. We didn't even include a mail order blank!*

This turned out to be a remarkably good catalogue, however, and it was a much better designed book than many of those that followed it. As a result of courses I had taken at Harvard in the history of the printed book, I had very strong convictions that legibility take precedence over all other elements. We learned very early that any design or layout that interferes with the ability of the eye to read the type easily and quickly and identify the copy with the picture will reduce buying response. This experience is one we have repeatedly passed on to new art directors, for many of them, in the desire to be creative, tend to ignore this basic principle of legibility.

This catalogue set a standard not only for quality and value, but for taste, editing, and ingenuity as well. Forty-three years later, the merchandise in the 1939 catalogue looks so good and timeless that it would be equally salable now. Shoulders on robes and jackets were puffed, following the influence of the French couturiere Schiaparelli. Lingerie was all made in pure unleaded silk, and gabardine was 100 percent wool. Then the synthetic revolution occurred!

Neiman-Marcus buyers came up with a

number of highly creative packaging ideas that produced sensational sales results. The Sports department presented a circular box with a clock face that housed three different sweaters, one each for morning, noon, and night, for a total price including the box of $11.95. Thousands of these packages were sold, taxing the capacity of our local boxmaker to keep us in supply.

The Man's Shop designed a special tie-a-day package containing seven assorted pure silk ties, one for each day of the week, for an all-inclusive price of $10.

In an effort to stimulate the handkerchief business, we created dolls with whimsical, hand-painted, wooden heads, dressed with three or four plain or printed handkerchiefs. The one in the form of a Christmas angel sold for $2.35, and the one shaped like a cowboy went for $1.85. These proved so successful that they became the mainstay of the N–M handkerchief business for many years. They were made in our stockrooms by a staff of handkerchief doll specialists, and their product was so charming that the copies brought out by the competition failed to have any effect on the sale of the originals.

That year we introduced our quilted satin-covered Treasure Chest box, free with the purchase of multiple gifts totaling a minimum of $100. This proved to be one of the most successful of all Neiman-Marcus gift package innovations. It encouraged the customer to put together an imaginative assortment of gifts to give greater satisfaction to the recipient. It also

Prices of the merchandise in the catalogue reflect the deflated values of the Depression years. A four-string simulated pearl necklace was priced at $2. A Steuben fluted bowl was $6. Steuben water goblets were $30 per dozen, and a Steuben flared vase was $15. Silverplate-on-copper service plates were $125 per dozen. A Georg Jensen acorn-patterned steak knife and fork set was $30. A seventeen-piece Irish linen, Swiss organdy luncheon set, hand embroidered in Madeira by Marghab, was $35. A Lenox swan-shaped salt and pepper set sold for $1.

increased the size of our average sale. This was in keeping with the credo of the store, "No sale is a good sale for Neiman-Marcus unless it is a good buy for the customer." The Treasure Chest became the epitome of the deluxe gift for the years of its existence. We refused to give it unless the rule of a purchase of two or more gifts was followed, and we never sold it separately, regardless of customer requests.

It should be observed that our economy was just emerging from the Depression, and these prices reflect the low levels of labor costs prevailing in 1939, which enabled us to come up with many creative packaging ideas that became prohibitively expensive in later years.

N–M's first simulated fur garment appeared in this book in the form of a furry robe with the copy "looks like ermine." If you think that a self-winding watch is relatively new, you are mistaken. You would have found it in the 1939 catalogue, shock resistant and waterproof, with a luminous dial at $29.75. Chinese checkers was described as "the game that has swept the country" at $10, and a walnut-finished, folding game table, a copy of an eighteenth-century model, went for $6.50. Actually, it wasn't successful until it was presented several years later as a TV snack table, at which time it sold by the thousands. We introduced a trick drinking glass that was so shaped that whiskey floated on top of the water. We named it the "jigger chaser" and sold it for $4 a dozen and continued to sell for years, until its maker went out of business.

The 1939 catalogue was a success, and an unbroken line of annual Neiman-Marcus Christmas books has followed. During the next five years we were at war, and the catalogues reflected the mood of the times; emphasis was on gifts for the men in service and military influences surfaced in toys and fashions. Certain best-selling items disappeared from the pages as material and labor shortages began to be felt.

*T*he 1941 catalogue carried an editorial which read in part: "We feel the uncertainty of the times draws us closer together; it makes us feel that the cherished traditions are all the more worthy of preservation." This was the catalogue of the year of Pearl Harbor, and the editorial, written many months prior to that event, indicated our sensitivity to the war around us. In that year's catalogue, nylon stockings made their first appearance, selling for $2.95 as compared with silk stockings, which were offered at $1.35 per pair. The stocking copy prophetically read, "While our collections now are bounteous and you're sure to find the stockings you want for gifts, we cannot make promises for the future." Alligator bags were available at $39.95; a man's fine gabardine lounge suit sold for $50. The 10 percent federal luxury tax showed up for the first time, too. It was a wartime levy imposed by the government for the dual purpose of discouraging the purchase of non-essentials and raising revenues to fight the war.

Handkerchiefs

Monogrammed and "named"

for "person to person" gifts

FOR THE GENTLEMEN

17-A Hand monogrammed white handkerchiefs, with hand rolled hems, and corded edges. 3 for 3.00

17-B For his coat pocket, sober or bright colored border handkerchiefs with hand rolled hems. .65 Or white hand-done initial handkerchief. .65

17-C The Gambler's Vest, one of our famous gift wraps in the Gay Nineties spirit. In it are three .65 men's white handkerchiefs. Complete, 2.20

FOR THE LADIES

17-D "Name" handkerchiefs are wonderful presents to find under your tree. Complete name, machine embroidered on sheer white hankies in color or white. Boxed and ribbon tied. 6 for 2.00

17-E Hand-embroidered monograms, any color, on sheer white handkerchiefs are welcome. 3 for 2.55

17-F Exquisite flower embroidered handkerchief, unusual "blossoming" petal effect. Pastels. 1.25

17-G Our famous "Handkerchief Doll" is Mrs. Gay Nineties herself. In four white or colored .65 women's handkerchiefs, she is complete. 2.95

Important: All names and monograms must be ordered before December 15th for Christmas delivery!

Neiman-Marcus Handkerchief Shop, First Floor

For glamour's sake . . . the FLORADORA GIFT WRAP. 25c extra with stockings. Holds two or three pairs, and hangs on her Christmas tree

Fine Neiman-Marcus Stockings

MORE TREASURED THAN EVER BEFORE

Exquisite sheer stockings, traditionally a cherished gift, are this year more appreciated than ever. For silks cannot be replaced in our stocks, and Nylons may be limited in the future. While our collections now are bounteous, and you're sure to find the stockings you want for gifts, we cannot make promises for the future. So we say, "Don't delay, order stockings now, while stocks are plentiful."

Fine Silk Chiffons 1.35 pair

All silk from top to toe
Two thread for dress
Three thread for daytime
"*Lazy Smoke*", warm taupe for black, blues, red.
"*Brown Beige*", cinnamon for browns, green.

Sheer Lovely Nylons 1.95 pair

For daytime wear
"*Lazy Smoke*", to wear with black, blues, red.
"*Wings*", taupe for black
"*Henny Penny*" for browns, green.

Sheerest of Nylons 2.95 pair

For dress wear
Black, glamorous for evening
"*Moor Mist*", deep taupe for black
Black-brown for black or brown
"*Conga*", skin tone for evening white

To help her keep her hosiery safely . . .
Glove and Hosiery Box
Just imagine her excitement if you filled this box with hosiery for her! Covered in quilted rayon satin in peach, turquoise, French blue, or rose dust. 1.50

In 1942, the editorial foreword recommended the purchase of government war bonds as a patriotic duty and as a share in our country's victory

A CHRISTMAS STORY
by
NEIMAN-MARCUS

Now—take the case
the service mar

B-21 Smooth suntan leather kit wit
toilet fittings, good brushes. Conve
size. Leather Shop, First Floor.

B-22 Remington Foursome, the su
electric razor with four cutting he
Neiman-Marcus Man's Shop. 1

B-23 A very handsome kit comple
equipped with everything he ne
Hazel pigskin, suede lined, e
pocket. Leather Shop, First Floor. 3

FOR THIS WARTIME CHRISTMAS
Neiman-Marcus can suggest no finer gift than a
Government War Bond—a share in our
country's victory. That patriotic duty done, we
turn to the glowing excitement of giving—the
spirit of Christmas that will always flame brightly.
Our Christmas-store is full of fantasy;
our fairylike decorations are "out of this world"
in their whimsy and delicacy . . . like the
dream of a child.
To help you keep your Christmas spirit,
we send you our 1942 Christmas Book, brimming
with lovely gifts. But this year, we urge you to
order early, for quantities are strictly limited
in many cases and reorders are impossible.
However, you'll find us abounding in suggestions,
and our exclusive gift wraps are as gay as ever.
We firmly believe, you see, that there'll
always be a Christmas!

NEIMAN-MARCUS

*For your little girl's room,
we suggest you frame the
quaint little maids on our cover,
painted by Elsie Shaver*

Like Polly, like Dolly
A-11 Polly wears our pinafore dress, blue, maize,
or pink with inset-white-pinafore. Toddler sizes
1 to 3, 6.95; 3 to 6, 7.95; 7, 8, 10, 8.95
A-12 Our matching Dolly, 3.95
The Red-White-Blue Christmas package. Gratis with gifts 8.95
or over; .20 extra below 8.95

Christmas IS FOR CHILDREN

Christmas —FOR ALL OUR MEN

Christmas —FOR LOVELY LADIES

Christmas —FOR BEAUTIFUL HOMES

Christmas IS FOR ONE AND ALL AT NEIMAN-MARCUS

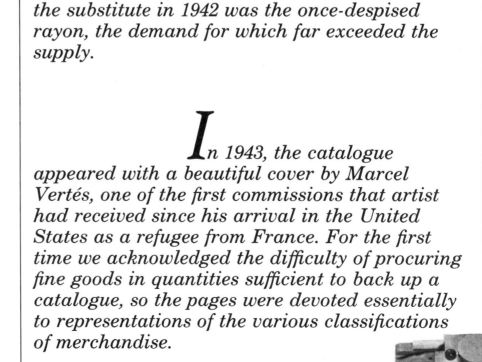

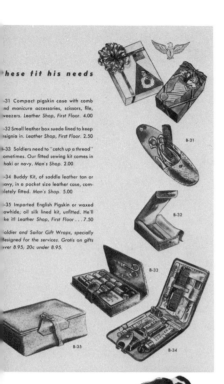

hese fit his needs

-31 Compact pigskin case with comb
nd manicure accessories, scissors, file,
weezers. Leather Shop, First Floor. 4.00

-32 Small leather box suede lined to keep
nsignia in. Leather Shop, First Floor. 2.50

-33 Soldiers need to "catch up a thread"
ometimes. Our fitted sewing kit comes in
haki or navy. Man's Shop. 2.00

-34 Buddy Kit, of saddle leather tan or
avy, in a pocket size leather case, com-
letely fitted. Man's Shop. 5.00

-35 Imported English Pigskin or waxed
owhide, oil silk lined kit, unfitted. He'll
ke it! Leather Shop, First Floor . . . 7.50

oldier and Sailor Gift Wraps, specially
esigned for the services. Gratis on gifts
ver 8.95; 20c under 8.95.

*I*n 1942, the editorial foreword recommended the purchase of government war bonds as a patriotic duty and as a share in our country's victory. The toys of that year were all martially inspired, with bomber planes and tanks in preponderance. A child's topcoat was cut in officer style and shown with an overseas cap. Also prominent in this issue were pages devoted to gifts for "the service man," including ID bracelets, officers' trench coats, and buddy kits. American-made China was a featured item; and while silk gowns at $9.95 to $14.95 were still available, gowns of rayon made their debut. No longer were nylon or silk stockings available, so the substitute in 1942 was the once-despised rayon, the demand for which far exceeded the supply.

*I*n 1943, the catalogue appeared with a beautiful cover by Marcel Vertés, one of the first commissions that artist had received since his arrival in the United States as a refugee from France. For the first time we acknowledged the difficulty of procuring fine goods in quantities sufficient to back up a catalogue, so the pages were devoted essentially to representations of the various classifications of merchandise.

1943

and War Bonds,
the best gift of all

Neiman-Marcus

1944

1945

Neiman-Marcus Christmas 1945

*I*n 1944, the new Neiman-Marcus Fine Jewelry department received its first catalogue notice with a double-page spread of precious jewelry for both women and men. This catalogue, produced at the time that governmental price ceilings had been placed on merchandise by the Office of Price Administration, carried a statement on its cover, "No price for any article listed herein exceeds the ceiling price. A statement of our maximum prices will be furnished upon request—Neiman-Marcus." Because of the necessity of adhering to OPA prices, odd-cent figure prices appeared for the first and only time in a Neiman-Marcus catalogue. Rayon stockings were advertised at $.96 and $1.17. The luxury tax this year was 20 percent, double that for the preceding year. Retailers were fearful that this levy would destroy the demand for the articles so taxed, but the demand in no way diminished.

*T*he 1945 catalogue displayed another joyous Vertés cover. The editorial that year read, "Merry Christmas. The fond wish will carry fuller note of joy this historic Peace Year of 1945. Families will be reunited. Children will have their 'Santa Claus' home. Christmas will be Christmas again." The catalogue was a full one, carrying wide

Customers were hungry for fine-quality European merchandise, unavailable in any quantity since 1939

Christmas Harlequinade, a treasury of gifts magically endowed with all the gaiety of the season. In these pages thirty wonderful suggestions from a store filled with all that is wonderful, all that is Christmas. A merry Neiman-Marcus Christmas to you!

Neiman

1946

please open before christmas

assortments of gifts at prices that were just beginning to show inflationary signs. An alligator bag this year sold for $59, and hosiery was notable by its absence. Since Texas was still a dry state, padded fabric bottle guards for those who carried booze to the restaurants sold for $2.25 in the quart size.

*I*n 1946, the catalogue's assortments showed that the war was truly over. Scotch cashmere sweaters were available for the first time since the war at $15.95 to $19.95. Hermès gloves in calfskin were $16.25. Orrefors crystal bowls from Sweden were offered at $13.90, and elaborately beaded bags from

France were advertised at $59, which included the 20 percent federal tax. Customers were hungry for fine-quality European merchandise, which had been unavailable in any quantity since 1939.

*T*he catalogues for this period were mostly in a large format measuring twelve by nine inches. In 1947, however, a new production manager decided to change the shape and design of the catalogue. Three catalogues published in 1947, 1948, and 1949 were the work of a talented young woman from Louisiana, Madeleine Pilgreen-Treadgold. She produced, in my opinion, three of the most charming catalogues that ever bore the N–M imprint. They were smaller in format, averaging eight by nine inches. The items were presented with large photographs, one or two to the page, and an order blank printed on the reverse side. This marked the first time Neiman-Marcus recognized that order blanks helped produce mail orders. Then, in 1949, dimensions were given on a number of articles. These two innovations were important in the history of the catalogue's evolution.

A catalogue first for 1949 was a pure silk twill necktie that could be personalized with two initials neatly embossed. No one on the editorial staff liked the idea, but the customers did. This item became so popular that it lived through two decades of catalogues.

As a sidelight of values of those few postwar years, a Steuben pitcher measuring eight and one-half inches in height was offered at $25 in 1947, and a Steuben bowl, six and one-half inches in diameter, was similarly priced in 1949. The price remained the same, but the size of the product shrunk.

a volume of gifts, with our best wishes for your happiest Christmas...

ONE EXQUISITELY BEAUTIFUL CULTURED ... TOPPED BY A DIAMOND, IN A 14 K. ... RING MOUNTING. WEAR ONE, WEAR TWO, ... OF THREE. 120.00 EACH, INCL. TAX. ... JEWELS, FIRST FLOOR

FABULOUS SILKS, WOVEN BY A FAMILY OF FAMOUS FRENCH WEAVERS, IN THREE HANDSOME TIES MADE WITH HAND-ROLLED EDGES. EACH DESIGN IN A TWO-COLOR COMBINATION: BROWN/BLUE BROWN/CHAMPAGNE, BLUE/RED, SILVER/BLUE, BLUE/WHITE, OR MAROON/WHITE MAN'S STORE, FIRST FLOOR

COOKBOOK PLUS IS "TASTE OF TEXAS," EDITED BY NEIMAN-MARCUS' OWN JANE TRAHEY AND JUST PUBLISHED BY RANDOM HOUSE. CONTAINS MORE THAN 300 UNUSUAL RECIPES, TESTED BY TEXAS STATE COLLEGE FOR WOMEN. FUN TO COOK BY, FUN TO READ. 3.00 EPICURE BAR, FIRST FLOOR

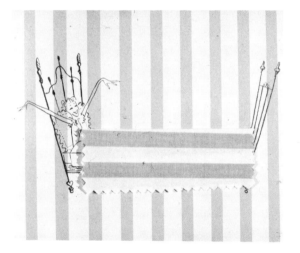

*P*eriodically, there were arguments and discussions in the advertising department about the ideal shape of a Christmas catalogue. The art directors usually wanted a large page for better presentation of photographs and copy. Buyers believed that a catalogue should be small enough to be carried in a woman's purse, so that she could then take it with her when she went to the store to do her Christmas shopping. In 1950, the proponents of the latter point of view won out, for the catalogue of that year shrank in size to seven by five inches.

This catalogue had two unusual gifts developed by members of the N–M buying and merchandising staff. One was woven candy-striped bed sheets and pillowcases, a radical departure from the solid colors then being used. This idea came from our merchandise manager, Joe Ross, who convinced the Wamsutta Mills to make these sheets exclusively for Neiman-Marcus. It took courage for Joe Ross to buy the huge quantities required by the manufacturer for an exclusivity on an unproven item. It proved to be an inspiring example for subsequent buyers and merchants to follow. An actual "feeler" swatch, three and one-half by two and one-half inches, was tipped into the book. Prior to their catalogue appearance, they were first introduced in the New York Times (incidentally, the first time a Neiman-Marcus advertisement appeared in that

90

Merry Christmas for her
in a nut shell! Literally! A pair of
soft, soft ostrich gloves —
so supple that each can be fitted
into a single walnut shell.
They're natural in color, all
hand sewn, and hand stitched in
black. The be-ribboned
shells make a most mysterious gift
to hang on the tree.
Glove sizes 6, 6½, 7, 7½.
10.50 complete.
Glove Shop, First Floor

paper). The Times, *which was rationing space at that time, was reluctant to accept advertising from an out-of-city store, and it was only after great persuasion that they agreed to carry it.*

There was a second creative accomplishment in this catalogue. When our glove buyer, Wilma Porter, made her first trip to Europe, she was impressed by some beautiful ostrich-skin gloves, which the manufacturer described to her as "being so soft and supple that a glove could be packed in a walnut shell." She responded by asking, "Why not? Let's pack them that way for the Neiman-Marcus Christmas catalogue." The manufacturer got himself into a jam, for while it was true that the gloves could be packed in the manner he had suggested, only those skins that came from the baby ostriches were thin enough to be used. Consequently, he had to go through scores and scores of skins to select the ones for the Neiman-Marcus walnut shell packing. Then, after they were made, his skilled glove makers refused to pack them, saying that this was out of their line of expertise. So the buyer and her assistant had to spend most of December hand-packing the gloves. The gloves packed in a walnut shell obviously had great news value and were publicized widely in the national press.

POSTMASTER: If undeliverable as addressed, notify sender stating reason or

*F*eature items in the 1951 catalogue were vicuña coats, a pair of initialed sterling silver diaper pins for $5, and stacked stool/tables for $29.50 for four. These were designed by Alvar Aalto, the Finnish architect whose work was just beginning to come to America at that time. Due credit was not given to Aalto, for in all probability the buyer had no knowledge who Aalto was.

I had always been a fan of Saul Steinberg and his wonderful New Yorker *magazine covers and cartoons. In 1950, it occurred to me that it would be a great coup if we could get him to*

THE NEIMAN-MARCUS CHRISTMAS BOOK

We also introduced the Flaminaire cigarette lighter from France, the first butane lighter to be marketed in the United States. "His and Her" gifts were represented by "His and Her" vicuña coats at $695 and "His and Her" Swiss watches at $90 and $145. On the "$5 and Under" pages, customers could order a snowman handkerchief at $4.50, a large initialed silk square scarf from Switzerland at $2.95, and Masslinn initialed cocktail napkins at $3.50 for a box of one hundred. A "feeler" sample of the napkin was bound into the catalogue.

*I*n 1951 we featured a white kidskin glove with a suede bluebird appliquéd in the palm of the left hand. The idea for this item came by sheer chance one night when I was visiting Dore Schary, the motion picture director and producer at MGM. At dinner that evening, one of the daughters, fifteen-year-old Jill, told me that she was studying costume design and wondered if I would take a look

at her sketches. I went through them and was very much impressed by her remarkable talent. Among the drawings was an idea for a glove based on the old proverb, "A bird in the hand is worth two in the bush." I told her that I thought this had commercial possibilities and asked if she wanted to sell the idea to us. She was delighted. We paid her a fee plus royalty on every pair of gloves sold. The item proved very successful at $12.95.

design a Christmas catalogue cover and gift-wrap paper as well. I approached his agent to see if she thought Steinberg would accept such a commission. She replied, "You never can tell about him. Why don't you go to his studio and ask him?" I did that and made a deal for the cover and the gift-wrap paper for $1,500, which was the highest price we had ever paid. He drew a charming Santa Claus, on which he pasted a beard of genuine green leaves and a red felt hat with a tassel dangling from it. We didn't think it safe to distribute a catalogue with a collage of fragile leaves, so we printed the beard and tipped on the felt hat. Both the cover and the gift-wrap paper proved to be a big hit. Steinberg was unhappy over the gift packages because, he said, "I don't like the idea of people tearing up my drawings." When I heard of his dissatisfaction, I wrote to tell him how many people he had pleased with his charming paper; instead of being upset that the papers were torn up, he should feel happy that he had given pleasure to so many people.

This was the first year in which we featured "His and Her" gift suggestions, but it is interesting to observe that this concept made no impact on the market. Only later, when we started developing esoteric "His and Her" gifts, did it register with the public and the press. The "His and Her" vicuña coats did impress a visiting Egyptian cotton merchant who made a special trip to Dallas to buy vicuña coats for his wife and himself, and for his four children, ranging in age from six to fifteen. He transformed the idea to "His and Theirs."

THE NEIMAN MARCUS CHRISTMAS BOOK

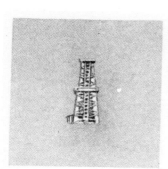

In the late forties, a new art director, Chuck Gruen, came to Neiman-Marcus. A talented designer with a great sense of fantasy, he brought a completely new advertising style to Neiman-Marcus newspaper advertising and to its Christmas catalogues. In the 1952 issue, with a cover featuring a pink-haired angel, there is a photograph of a woman dressed in our exclusive Pesante silk dress who looks just as chic today as she did in 1952. A Steuben crystal dish with curving scroll handles about eight inches in diameter sold for $25, and a Georg Jensen acorn-patterned sterling silver bottle opener retailed for $8.50 including tax. All gift wraps were gratis on purchases of $19.75 and over. Gift wraps under that price earned a charge of $.35.

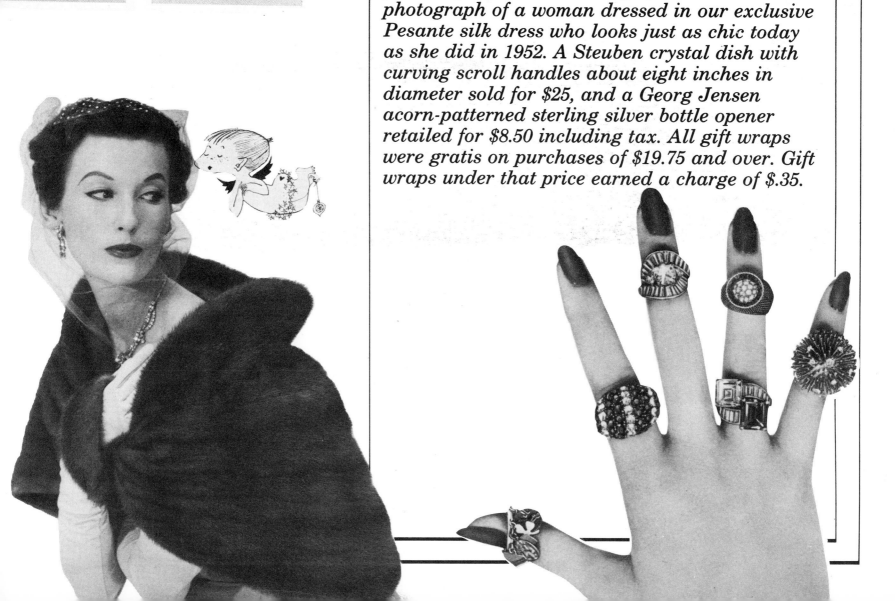

The 1953 catalogue cover was a charming and imaginative design, replete with the figure of an angelic-looking choir boy. Produced by rotogravure in an effort to reduce rising production costs it was distributed in a Sunday edition of the Dallas Morning News as well as by mail to the N–M charge customer list. This catalogue had a larger page format, but while well designed, it did not carry the connotation of quality that characterized earlier catalogues. Neiman-Marcus was becoming aware of Texas itself at this time, as indicated by a special cocktail tray reproducing various Texas commemorative coins, highball glasses decorated with oil well gushers, and a music box compact which played "The Eyes of Texas" when opened. This last item proved to be tremendously successful, with a demand for special tunes of other states and countries as well.

European merchandise began to appear more frequently as an increasing number of Neiman-Marcus buyers traveled to the European markets. In the 1953 catalogue, the Gift Shop introduced an item that would prove to be one of its greatest successes, a set of steak knives from France made of hand-forged stainless steel. Six knives in a box sold for $5.95. From England came a wooden crate of a dozen bars of soap made in the form and color of lemons. This eye-appealing gift retailed for $4.

THE NEIMAN MARCUS CHRISTMAS BOOK

*T*he 1954 catalogue came down in size but went up in the quality of both printing and paper stock. The cover feature was a Christmas character, the sugarplum fairy, who became the theme of the N–M Christmas promotion. A mannequin dressed in replica made appearances in the Zodiac restaurant every afternoon giving away sugarplum cookies to all the children. On the opening page of the catalogue was a sugarplum tree decorated with sugar-covered cookies in the shapes of the traditional barnyard animals. The "His and Her" gift motif which had appeared occasionally in the previous Neiman-Marcus catalogues came forth in 1954 in two pages. One was "His and Her" blotter robes inspired by the terry cloth peignoirs furnished by most European hotels and the other was "His and Her" pure silk dressing robes.

madeline fashions

Neiman-Marcus

*T*he cover of the 1955 catalogue was designed by Ludwig Bemelmans, the creator of the famous child character Madeline, for whom we designed and made a complete wardrobe for our customers' little girls. This catalogue marked first appearances in an N–M catalogue of a synthetic fur coat woven of a blend of Orlon and Dynel and stretch socks, knitted from a mixture of cashmere and nylon.

When I was in Europe in that year, I conceived the idea of developing a special color insert to be printed in Holland and bound into the regular catalogue. I was on a buying trip that started in Italy and ended in Sweden. I picked out the one item I thought was the most unusual gift of the year from each country. I selected among other things a velvet handbag by Roberta of Venice, which started a whole new fashion trend in handbags throughout the world. I had found the velvet in a Venetian textile mill specializing in the weaving of fabrics for the Vatican. Never before had they sold a piece of cloth to be used in trade. Roberta, who lived in Venice, was unfamiliar with this mill but was delighted to see a piece of velvet that looked as though it might have come from the days of the Renaissance and agreed to experiment with it. Also in this special section was a cigarette box and paperweight by Piero Fornasetti, the great graphic designer of Milan.

Some years previously, I had made a collection of the prints of tradesmen by L'Armessin, an eighteenth-century French engraver. I took half a dozen of them to Switzerland, where we had them printed on a thirty-six-inch silk square. This scarf, which was the first in a series we called "The Library of Fashion Scarfs," retailed for $16.95.

The special catalogue insert was printed by the venerable firm of Enschedé and Zöhnen of Haarlem, Holland. This company was the oldest and foremost printer in the Netherlands, doing everything from catalogue work to printing the Dutch currency and postal stamps. It also performed a similar service for some seventy-five other nations in the world. In order to make our schedule, the inserts had to be shipped by July 1 from Holland to reach the United States in time to be bound in with the rest of the catalogue. The printer delivered on time, but a dock strike in the U.S. held up the shipment in Galveston for four weeks. When it was finally released, we found that the heat in the hold of the ship had caused many of the pages to become stuck together. After great effort, we succeeded in separating the pages and barely made the time schedule to ensure delivery of the Christmas catalogue on time. The resulting catalogue was beautiful, but it taught us the lesson never to gamble on a printing job outside of the country, particularly if there was a Christmas deadline.

I had a good friend in New York, Bill Weintraub, head of a successful national advertising agency, who took a great interest in the Neiman-Marcus catalogue and voluntarily critiqued it every year. Following the 1955 catalogue, he told me: "You are making a great mistake not to make more capital of your unique gift-wrapped packages. You have something that nobody else in the country does so well, and you ought to put them

on the cover of your catalogue or at least in a double-page spread in the center." We took his advice; and in 1956, the front and back covers reproduced the Neiman-Marcus gift-wrapped packages. This year, the price for gift wraps had gone up to $.50 and were gratis on gifts over $100. Bill Weintraub's advice proved correct, for the demand for gift-wrapped packages doubled.

The 1956 book contained a couple of dramatic pages which were the forerunners of the big breakthrough in 1960. My brother Edward thought up the idea of decorating a Steiff plush tiger with precious jewels, bringing the gift up to a value of one million dollars. This made national news and was picked up by Life magazine, which reproduced it in its Christmas roundup story. On the page facing the $1,000,000 gift was a baby tiger with a Saint Christopher charm on a gold bracelet priced at $100, which of course didn't interest Life. We didn't sell any $1,000,000 gifts, but we did sell hundreds of baby tigers.

This catalogue presented a deluxe tool cabinet, made by London's Asprey of Bond Street, which was a superb and extravagant gift for the time; it was priced at $550, an unheard-of amount for a set of carpenter tools. At the other end of the spectrum, we featured an Italian sterling silver thimble decorated with semiprecious stones at $2.50, which sold by the thousands. One customer came to me looking for a suggestion of a gift to send to a royal

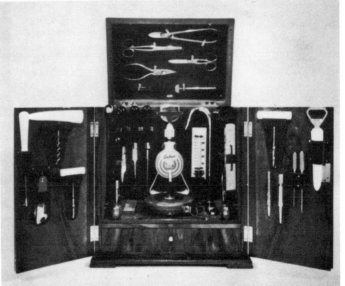

*O*ne order came in from a seven-year-old boy:

Dear Mr. Neiman Marcus, How much is your Life tiger? Not the diamonds. I am a tiger collector, not diamonds. I am seven, and I have five tigers. Not real, just play. I love tigers, especially yours. Please send the letter and how much it costs without the diamonds right away. Also, can you charge it or do you have to pay right away? I have my garden money, so please send the letter right away before I lose it.

Your friend,*

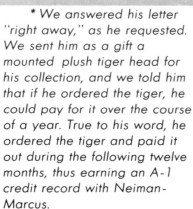

* We answered his letter "right away," as he requested. We sent him as a gift a mounted plush tiger head for his collection, and we told him that if he ordered the tiger, he could pay for it over the course of a year. True to his word, he ordered the tiger and paid it out during the following twelve months, thus earning an A-1 credit record with Neiman-Marcus.

*T*here was a mink handbag by Nettie Rosenstein at $395, N-M perfume at $110 for two ounces, lorgnette opera glasses made of cloisonné and mother-of-pearl at $82.50, and a lamé handbag from India set with large cabochon rubies, sapphires, and emeralds at $750.

*T*he 1957 catalogue shopper could order anything from a diamond necklace for $24,750 and a mink cape at $2,750 to a three-way silver Italian pill box for $2.95, an English bone china sugar and creamer set on a small tray for $4.95, and a leather-covered pocket tape at $1.95. It also introduced *Helen Corbitt's Cookbook,* written by the director of the Neiman-Marcus Zodiac restaurant, which proved over the years to be one of the largest sellers that the catalogue ever had.

princess in Europe. He said he couldn't afford to spend very much, but he wanted to send some token of esteem. I recommended the silver thimble, which proved to be exactly the right thing, because it fit both his pocketbook and the occasion. This catalogue continued to feature large assortments of goods from Western Europe, as those markets regained their strength and eminence. There is little doubt that our consistent support of small mills and producers, through selections of their products for inclusion in our catalogue, provided great encouragement to craftsmen in the postwar period.

In 1956, for the first time the N-M Christmas catalogue was copyrighted. This action was an obvious response to the fact that the competition was copying layouts and even sketches.

*F*or the fiftieth anniversary *of Neiman-Marcus, in 1957, a special page was devoted to "A Golden World of Fashion," in which gifts from all over the world had been gathered together in celebration of the occasion.*

*T*he gift wraps occupied a full page on the frontispiece of the 1958 catalogue. They were priced at $.50 each or gratis on a gift of $100 or more. This catalogue had a new art director, for it is obvious that the layouts were very much different from those of preceding years.

We originated a stunning mink stole made from ombréd beige to brown mink. Also for the first time in the catalogue were sports clothes by Emilio Pucci, the Florentine designer who did so much to revolutionize the fashion color palette in the latter part of the fifties. His printed scarf shirts and brightly colored, form-fitting pants in two-way stretch Helenca were great winners at $55 each and became status symbols at the beginning of an era when women responded to articles bearing designers' signatures.

The "Neiman-Marcus Model Smock" was launched in the catalogue for the first time in 1958. It shared a page with another garment, since neither the buyer nor the art director had any idea that it would prove to be the biggest-selling apparel item that Neiman-Marcus had ever catalogued. It sold for $25.95, and orders were received from stage and movie celebrities such as Ethel Merman, Helen Hayes, and Ina Claire, leading fashion mannequins, and hundreds of housewives who thought the garment met their requirements equally well.

The Library of Fashion scarf was printed with reproductions of horses in famous

paintings and was priced now at $17.95. One of the paintings, all of which we thought were in the public domain, turned out to be in the private collection of a gentleman in Switzerland who took exception to our reproduction of his painting on a silk scarf. Fortunately, we were able to adjudicate the matter with him to his satisfaction by giving him a dozen scarfs and by agreeing not to reprint it. A bar towel printed on pure linen in Ireland, reproducing the credo of the Benedictine monks at $2, sold into the thousands. This was inspired by a broadside by one of San Francisco's leading book printers, John Henry Nash. It proved so successful that it is still in print, twenty-five years later.

Following the 1955 success of Bemelmans' Madeline and her special wardrobe, the 1958 catalogue presented Kay Thompson's inimitable character Eloise, with a wardrobe of dresses, a terry robe, and bath towels embroidered with a design from one of Hilary Knight's charming drawings.

This year marked the end of an era, in which time we produced catalogues for the sale of merchandise by mail. We had improved our techniques of presentation so that our readers could find all the information as to size, weight, and colors necessary for easy shopping. In the following years, the N–M catalogue made news as well as sales and became a powerful selling tool, both to publicize the store and to add new customers to our mailing lists.

Chapter 4
★
A NEW ERA BEGINS

During its first fifty years, Neiman-Marcus attracted national attention because of its success as a distributor of fine-quality merchandise in what was then considered remote Texas. National publications had run feature stories about this unusual store, "deep in the heart of . . ." Additional interest was fanned by Texas stories emanating from Texans in the armed services and from the wartime immigrants to Texas. Neiman-Marcus had used some unorthodox publicity techniques for calling the public's attention to its city and to its business, such as super spectacular fashion shows, gift-wrapped packages, VIP red carpet treatment, and other devices.

*W*e found that originality paid off as more people from outside the borders of Texas began to order by mail. Finally in 1959, when Neiman-Marcus made its first public sale of common stock, a helpful stockbroker, Ted Birr of San Francisco, urged further development of the mail order arm of the business. This suggestion was acted upon, and a new philosophy—Neiman-Marcus by mail—was born. Under the direction of Edward Marcus, we expanded both the mailing lists and the number of publications. The circulation of the Christmas catalogue, which up to that time had been 250,000, was jumped to 500,000. The 1959 catalogue proved to be a forerunner of our explosive new Neiman-Marcus Christmas catalogues.

Edward, who raised prize black Angus cattle, thought it would be a great idea to offer a black Angus steer in our catalogue. Although a cow in a Neiman-Marcus catalogue was an obvious absurdity, it was not quite droll enough. As I was searching for some twist to add a degree of whimsy, I recalled the large silver-plated carts that were used in London restaurants like Scott's and Simpson's. The photograph of the steer and the cart produced a tremendous amount of publicity, particularly when we were able to reveal after Christmas that we had received several orders, including one from a customer in Sacramento, California, who made us swear that we wouldn't disclose her purchase of the gift until after Christmas.

I suggested that we photograph the black Angus steer on the hoof together with a roast beef chart. We priced the two with a Texas gift wrap ("gift wrapped as best we can," we said) for $1,925, f.o.b., Chicago. Then, to give the item a real kicker, we offered our "tenderfoot friends" the steer cut into 300 pounds of steaks, roast, ground beef, etc., with the cart, for $2,230 f.o.b., Chicago.

However, she couldn't keep her own mouth shut, for she told the story to Louella Parsons, the columnist, who made the most of it. The second order came from South Africa. We shipped the steer and the cart, but when they arrived in South Africa, we learned to our great consternation that livestock had to be kept in quarantine for six months before being admitted to the country. That meant that we had to feed and board the steer in Johannesburg until the following July, when we were able to make delivery. The money we lost on the charges we made up in the international publicity the story brought.

The finale of the book was an extravaganza I concocted that unfortunately missed the mark. It was a photograph of a pink Jeep with a fringed surrey top at $1,848, f.o.b., Dallas. Along with the Jeep was what we called a "Dash of Luxury," which really added up—an Empress chinchilla coat, cabochon emerald and diamond earrings, and a diamond necklace. Those little tidbits, seasoned with a hibachi grill, a champagne bucket, Baccarat champagne glasses, a transistor TV, and a gourmet's food basket, were photographed on a romantic beach. The total was $151,580.70.

It was a constant struggle to maintain the balance of a catalogue that would be read by hundreds of thousands of customers scattered all over the world. We wanted to present the new, but we could never afford to be so completely new that conservative readers might feel left out. We had to maintain a range of prices

*C*ome-as-you-are
beach party extravaganza

so that there would be worthy items within the buying power of almost any customer. We had to balance gifts by age groups to satisfy those who wanted something for Grandmother as well as for a teenage daughter. Along with this balancing process, we had to select a merchandise mix that would sell, one that would justify the kind of dollar investment necessary to ensure our ability to fulfill a high percentage of orders.

During our first twenty years of cataloguing, we featured gift merchandise ranging from fashion accessories to crystal and silver and from children's clothes to furs. We wanted to emphasize our position as the pre-eminent gift store of the nation; besides which, customer returns on such objects were relatively low. Gift merchandise stayed sold! We knew from experimenting that apparel, with all of the complications of fit and attractiveness, was subject to a very high rate of return. Nonetheless, the temptation of higher unit prices for dresses and coats and the sales volume such items could produce prompted us to try to find a way to offset costs that a 25 percent return ratio would cause.

We discovered that if we anticipated the returns, reduced our initial purchases proportionately, and then staggered our mailings by a few weeks, we could fill later orders from the returns generated by the sales of the earlier mailings. We started off with classic sports separates and gradually enlarged our selections into sports dresses and topcoats.

*F*or several years, we had been receiving phone calls a week or so before Christmas from Ed Murrow of CBS or his young associate, Walter Cronkite, and from other network commentators who were doing Christmas roundup stories. "What is the big Christmas item this year?" was the invariable question. Some years we had an exciting story—as, for example, the time a man purchased the entire contents of the corner show window on the condition that we would reproduce it in the playroom of his home on Christmas Eve. Or the tale of the man who came in and bought five mink coats for his five daughters and a sable coat for his wife.

We avoided seasonal fabrics such as velveteen and lamé, and this worked very well for the customers and the store. We moved into dressier clothes and shoes, but we stayed away from very high fashion apparel with which the customers were unlikely to have had previous experience.

The mail order success of clothes for both women and men proved to be a turning point in our catalogue history. Our volume skyrocketed with higher average orders as our customers bought clothes for themselves as well as for gifts. Transactions increased to the point that we were forced to use not only the computer but also other electronic order-filling devices to maintain our efficiency.

The introduction of fashion apparel brought other problems that we had to solve. Since the fashion publications such as Vogue *and* Harper's Bazaar *used top photographers for the display of clothes, we felt forced to switch from sketches to top-quality photography. Leading photographers gave lower contract prices to the magazines than they quoted us. This forced us to search for new, undiscovered talent within our budget limitations.*

We were fortunate in having an exceptionally talented fashion director, Kay Kerr, whose taste and fashion judgment were as sharp as those of any magazine fashion editor. I once called her "the fashion conscience of Neiman-Marcus," for she was a perfectionist who would not accept an article of merchandise for the catalogue or approve a photograph if she believed there was a better solution. Some

artists and buyers found it difficult to work with her since she would not accept the compromises less exacting people were willing to make. She supervised the photography for all of our national fashion advertisements and most of the fashions in the catalogues for about twenty years; during her tenure we never had cause to be embarrassed by the standard of taste in model selection, accessorizing, or posing.

Among the new photographers she discovered were Wilbur Pippin and Hiro, now two of the most famous in the world. A careful examination of the hundreds of faces appearing in the catalogue reveals Lauren Hutton long before she reached stardom at Revlon. Suzy Parker, one of the most famous models in both Europe and America, appeared in the N-M Christmas book, as did Carmen and Wilhelmina. Wilhelmina subsequently established the fashion modeling agency bearing her name. Naomi Sims, who later started her own wig business, was also a model for us. Shelley Smith, later a film actress, modeled for us, as did Princess Elizabeth of Togo shortly after her arrival in the United States and prior to becoming her country's ambassador to the United Nations.

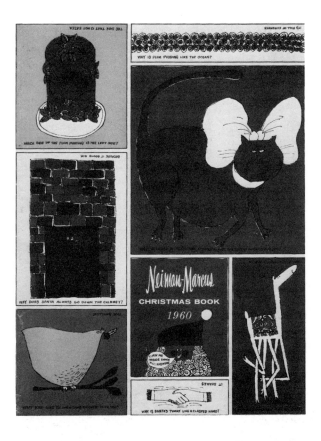

*I*t occurred to me that if we deliberately created unusual gifts and ran them in the catalogue, we'd not only answer the demands of the networks for exciting stories but we would simultaneously pick up coverage in most of the newspapers as well.

I threw out the challenge to our senior merchandising and promotional executives, asking each of them to come up with a proposal of an exciting, esoteric, newsworthy gift idea where salability was no question. I urged them to let their imaginations run rampant just as long as their proposals were in basic good taste.

One of our merchandise executives, David Hughes, came forth with the idea of "His and Her airplanes." This seemed preposterous to some of my associates, but I thought it had the newsworthy quality so essential to the success of the idea. We broached the idea with the Beech Aircraft Corporation in Wichita, Kansas, and they were delighted to accept our invitation to join in this presentation. This ran in our Christmas catalogue of 1960, along with another "idea" page—the complete Modern Library of Random House, suggested as reading material for anyone unfortunate enough to be a castaway on a desert island.

The theory was proved a success by the results. The catalogue was reported not only by the networks in this country but by the BBC and other radio and television stations all over Europe. In addition, we garnered thousands of inches of space in newspapers throughout the

*"**I** already have a plane, but if you will break the pair, I'd like one for the little woman, who has been hankering for a plane of her own"*

The 1960 catalogue opened with a dramatic presentation of gift-wrapped packages plus a new version of the Treasure Chest in the form of a three-foot Formosan wedding basket. A double-page color spread followed with the "His and Her" Beechcraft planes as a background for a formally attired couple dressed for anything but a plane flight. A rancher from west Texas wrote in, saying, "I can't use both planes, for I already have one I use for myself; but if you will break the pair, I'd like one for the little woman, who has been hankering for a plane of her own for a long time." We gladly acquiesced and painted her name, "Mamie Belle," on the nose as he had specified.

*I*f the
reader's fancy was not
taken by the "His and
Her" airplanes, there was
a sleeveless Empress chin-
chilla tunic designed by
Neiman-Marcus for
$7,500.

world, from Singapore to Alaska, from Maine to the Philippines. Immediately we began receiving calls for Christmas catalogues, and in a very short time the supply was exhausted.

We realized that we had a tiger by the tail: the success of this first year would require equally exciting concepts for the following years. The problem of topping the previous year's idea page became a very real and pressing one, and it taxed the imaginative ability of our entire organization. Many times we were able to come up with concepts in-house, but we were happy to accept suggestions from customers or suppliers who had novel gift approaches.

The great secret of Neiman-Marcus merchandising over the years has been its ability to provide both the finest expensive goods in the world and merchandise of equally good taste but moderately priced. This is exactly the technique that we applied to the catalogue, and we encountered the same success there as we had with the stores.

Neiman-Marcus

Ronald Searle

*T*he most exciting thing
about the 1961 catalogue was its cover, by the
English caricaturist-illustrator Ronald Searle.
It depicted a reindeer, in bed with his antlers
decorated for the annual Christmas trip, being
exhorted by Santa Claus to "get up and get
going." It was fondly referred to by the
advertising staff as "the reluctant reindeer."

As my catalogue experience grew, I began
to develop a philosophy as to the structure of

the book so that it would satisfy the needs and desires of the various types of readers. Our customers were of all ages, of different income levels, and from all parts of the country. The only thing they had in common was an appreciation of the taste and quality levels that Neiman-Marcus presented. To that end, I wanted to open with an assortment of "knock-them-dead" ideas that could satisfy the gift requirements of the most extravagant buyer, searching for something for "the man or woman who has everything." These gifts we labeled the "Superlatives" or "Incomparables."

Following the ever-growing popularity of the James Bond movies, Neiman-Marcus decided to do a little spoofing in this catalogue. On the inside cover we offered a special new confidential service for customers who send gifts to those in exceedingly high positions—kings, shahs, maharajas, prime ministers, and other heads of state.

We received one order for a gift to a head of state and seventeen orders for girlfriends and twenty-three for boyfriends. This tongue-in-cheek presentation was given widespread news coverage.

For reasons beyond my recollection, we failed to follow up on the successful "His and Her" planes that year. Instead, we had a couple of feature items which, though nice, in no way provided the same volume of publicity. We created a white full-length ermine bathrobe which, of course, could double as an evening wrap. It sold for $6,975 and was purchased by a customer living in Madrid, Spain.

*A*vailable this year for the first time was a monogrammed hammer for $8.95, a set of six green shamrock-decorated Irish coffee cups and saucers for $7.95, and a baker's dozen of men's handker-chiefs: thirteen handker-chiefs wrapped in a special package topped with a baker's *toque blanche*, all for $7.50.

We also featured a living room wall of wine with the offer to stock it with vintage wines for $5,000. This was at the beginning of American interest in wines; and while we had few takers for the whole "upstairs cellar," it materially helped the development of our wine business. There was a lightweight traveler's scale at $30, something I've been looking for ever since. Florence Eiseman designed a little girl's tutu, which produced orders from many parts of the world, including fifty from England's premier ballerina, to be sent to each of her god-daughters.

The prior success of blotter robes inspired us to make them available once again to our customers, this time with a three-letter monogram. This presentation pulled in over 3,000 orders and it became a staple in our stocks for many years.

To help relieve the monotony of intensive selling, we devised the tongue-in-check section "Things You Didn't Know You Needed Until Now."

The whimsy provided by that page seemed to me to be an important ingredient that helped distinguish our catalogue from those of the competition. Sometimes the section sold merchandise in quantity; other times it didn't. They were purposeful spoofs, and, of course, if readers didn't order, we hoped they would at least get a laugh. This feature made its first appearance in the 1962 book.

This sort of balance seemed to work well for us; people liked to buy a $10 gift from a store that had "His and Her" airplanes and $15,000 fur coats.

Annual buying trips to European markets were so time consuming that I never could fit in a trip to the Far East; in 1962, I finally managed to do both by going around the world. The impact of the journey and my merchandise discoveries showed up in the 1962 catalogue and those of the next few years.

A friend in Hong Kong entertained us on his Chinese junk one Sunday afternoon, and the experience persuaded me that a junk would be a marvelous feature for the book. We labeled it "Junk for Christmas" at $11,500, f.o.b., Houston. We had the foresight to require six months for delivery. Since the junk builders would provide no cooperative advertising support money, we photographed the vessel tied up to a pier loaded with appropriate nationally advertised products such as Sony, Vuitton luggage, and Baccarat stemware, all of which helped defray the advertising costs.

We located a junk in the Hudson River and produced a smashing color photograph for a double spread. To our amazement, we received eight orders to be delivered to five different bodies of water and more publicity than on any other feature item since the "His and Her" airplanes. Emilio Azcarraga, Jr., the television tycoon from Mexico, ordered one on the condition that we would provide someone to rig it for him. We located an experienced junk sailor who was honeymooning in Dallas. We pursuaded him to complete his honeymoon in

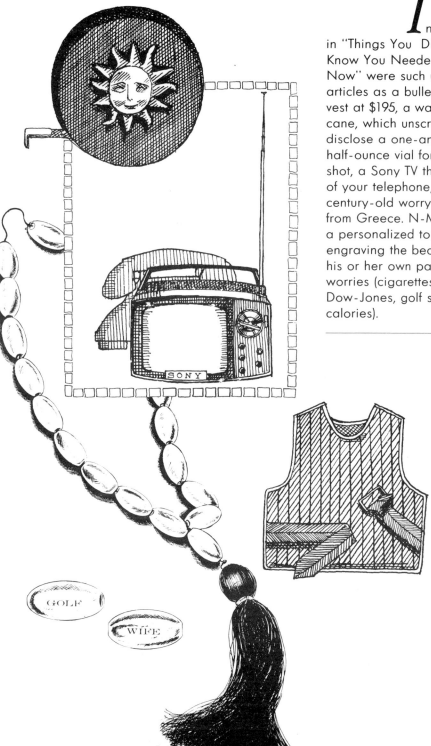

JUNK FOR CHRISTMAS

*I*ncluded in "Things You Didn't Know You Needed Until Now" were such useful articles as a bullet-proof vest at $195, a walking cane, which unscrewed to disclose a one-and-one-half-ounce vial for a quick shot, a Sony TV the size of your telephone, and century-old worry beads from Greece. N-M added a personalized touch by engraving the beads with his or her own particular worries (cigarettes, Dow-Jones, golf score, calories).

GOLF

WIFE

SONY

A Christmas doormat for $5 was produced by a local Junior Achievement group, but the volume of orders overwhelmed the young entrepreneurs. They could fill only 500 of the 2,500 orders, forcing us to send cancellation notices to 80 percent of the customers who had ordered.

Acapulco and flew him and his bride there, where he rigged the junk. The junk is still sailing in Mexican waters.

Mink was just then attaining the height of its popularity; so, to prove that we were, in fact, national headquarters for any- and everything made in mink, we made cowboy chaps in white mink at $1,875. We showed them in ensemble with white satin pants and a white satin cowboy shirt, a rhinestone-studded western belt, and white kidskin cowboy boots as an at-home cocktail outfit, anticipating the western fashion boom by a dozen years.

In 1963, we opened the book with a double-page spread of "His and Hers." For the man, we had a shahtoosh muffler made from the chin hairs of the ibex goat found in the Himalayan Mountains in Kashmir. It was and still is the finest fiber in the world. This luxurious muffler, which sold for $100 in 1963, would have to sell for $2,250 today. We even made a kimono robe in shahtoosh, which was shown on a man seated in the classic Charles Eames chair with its matching ottoman. For

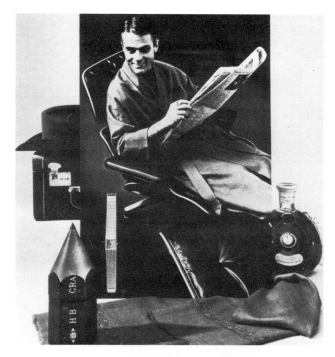

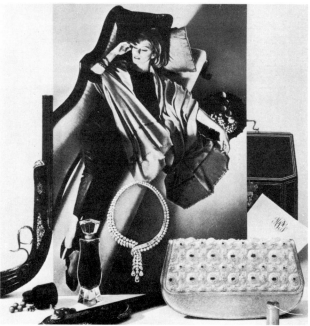

her, we showed the shahtoosh *stole that measured four and one-half feet by eight feet. This type of scarf represents to an Indian woman what a mink coat does to a woman in the West. Its texture is so fine that the whole stole can be pulled through a man's wedding ring, and from this fact it became known as a "ring scarf." From India was a bag woven of silver bullion threads and adorned with genuine sapphires—not of fine quality but effective enough for a bag and completely genuine.*

For the child who had everything, we found a railroad made in England of plastic and galvanized steel. It had enough track to set up a forty-eight-by-twenty-four-foot layout with additional trackage available. The rolling stock included an electric locomotive and a Pullman car in which six children could speed around the family grounds. It was priced at $1,500.

When I was in Japan that year visiting the Osaka Trade Fair, I walked for miles in the exhibition halls before finding a single thing I thought was salable for Neiman-Marcus. Finally, I came upon one item that paid for the trip. It was a metal strongbox with a combination lock and an alarm which sounded when the lid was opened. It had great appeal for little boys. It retailed for $20, and it became a staple in the Neiman-Marcus catalogue for about a dozen years.

The big "His and Her" item was a miniature submarine heralded as "The Ultimate in Togetherness." The copy read, "Designed to carry two people, it cruises at a

*T*he Ultimate in Togetherness

speed of 3 to 7.3 miles per hour. The slightly buoyant Mini Sub has a hull of plastic impregnated laminated glass cloth. 14 feet long, 46 inches high, 90 inches wide. It weighs 975 pounds. Battery operated. One horsepower motor. $18,700 f.o.b., Dallas."

On another page was shown a full-length white mink evening wrap at $7,950, accompanied by a superb necklace of diamonds and matched cat's eyes for $110,000. An order for the coat came to us from Monaco, and a customer traveled all the way from Boston to examine and eventually buy the necklace.

We devoted another double-page spread to a dramatic videotape television recorder which was the forerunner of today's very popular electronic devices. It included an Ampex videotape recorder, a home television camera and tripod, a television tuner, and an automatic timer, a television receiver, an automatic record turntable, an AM-FM multiplex, an Ampex stereo audiotape recorder, a stereo preamplifier control unit, transistorized power amplifiers, stereo loudspeaker system, and two professional microphones. It measured 108 inches long, 40 inches high, and 30 inches wide. It weighed approximately 900 pounds and sold for $30,000. One set was ordered by a prominent Hollywood star. Now, nineteen years later, components which would perform the same services can be bought for $6,837.

It seems the only articles that have moved counter to postwar inflation have been those that benefited from technological advances—

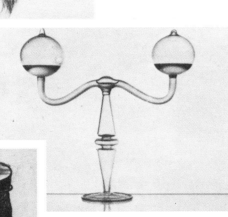

"**T**hings You Didn't Know You Needed Until Now" had such nonsense suggestions as a ten-gallon hat for a pet dog and a wastebasket made from an elephant foot at $350, the demand for which certainly exceeded our expectations. Finally, there was a glass passion meter from France, which we prudishly relabeled "A Temper Meter." The copy read, "By holding one of the glass bulbs, a person's temper can be measured." There was a run on these.

*F*or $5 and under, we offered five tubes of toothpaste flavored like brandy, martini, and orange curaçao. This gift suggestion was repulsive to me. I tried to fight it, but the selection committee voted me down. It proved to be one of our all-time popular items and, I have to admit, a version of it is still being sold with continuing success.

some as beneficiaries of the space program. Calculators, radios, TVs, watches, and other electronic devices are lower in price, higher in quality, and smaller in size than they were twenty years ago.

Credit cards were just coming into wide usage, and here for the first time we featured a credit card holder in alligator for $30. We found a golf swing analyzer that combined a graphic-check sequence camera with a Polaroid back, delivering the pictures in less than ten seconds. This retailed for $395. Also for the golf enthusiast, we had an electric putting game to sharpen up putting shots on winter days. This sold for $1,895 and had takers from all over the country.

That year, we initiated "Neiman-Marcus Every Month," a food plan that gave the recipient a different food gift every month for a price of $75. This proved to be highly productive and has been repeated every year since, reaching a price of $228 in 1981.

On reflection, I find this catalogue, with a cover designed by Bjørn Wiinblad of Denmark, to be filled with more innovative ideas than almost any other catalogue in the entire forty-year period. Perhaps more new things were coming on the market. Perhaps the Neiman-Marcus buyers tried harder that year to develop fresh, exciting, and tempting new ideas. Almost two decades later, it's still an exciting book to peruse.

*O*ur cover for 1964 was designed by another wonderful artist from Denmark, Ib Antoni. The cover had a profile of Santa Claus with a long white beard which birds were using as a ski run.

We followed my friend Weintraub's advice of putting the gift-wrapped packages up front in the book by placing them on the inside cover. Gift-wrap costs had increased to the extent that individual wraps went up to $.75 and $1 and were gratis with gifts over $100 and $150, respectively.

On the first page, we photographed the luxurious Greenhouse, a beauty and health spa located midway between Dallas and Fort Worth, which I described as "a hot-house for wilted ladies."

The "Things You Didn't Know You Needed Until Now" page was repeated for a third year with a fox-covered wastebasket at $30, a violin case which had been converted to carry a quart of whiskey, inspired in part by the liquor laws of Texas and by the gangsters' use of violin cases for carrying lethal weapons, and a black horn wife whistle from Austria for $2.50.

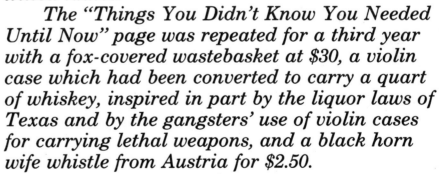

The "His and Her" gifts were hot air balloons in pink and white stripes powered by "pink air" provided by American Petrofina. The balloons were $6,850 each, including a pilot check-out. The hottest item of that year's catalogue, small six-and-one-half-inch cosmetic bags to be carried in the purse, were made in Italy from colorful cotton brocade, at $3.50. We delivered over 5,000, exhausting the manufacturer's supply of fabric.

his his hers hers

*M*odes of transportation
seemed to lend themselves most readily to the
development of exotic "His and Her" gifts. In
1965, we took inspiration from the Para-Sails,
first popularized at the La Concha Beach Club
of Las Brisas in Acapulco. It became a
double-page spread near the opening of the
book. So many people had been transported by
these devices in Acapulco that there was a
ready market for them. After Christmas,
Para-Sails appeared on many of the lakes
around the country.

Every year we have had supply difficulty
with a product for one reason or another.
Occasionally, we have bought a product which
upon delivery didn't work well. Such was the
case with "Peruna," a very realistic-looking
mechanical horse measuring thirty-nine inches
in height by thirty-five inches in length.

Peruna was ridden into the Christmas
selection meeting by the toy buyer who had
discovered him in Spain. It was a wonderful toy
any young child would love to have, and the
first samples we received worked perfectly.
Unfortunately, when our order for 400 horses
was delivered, we found that about half didn't
work well. Rather than take the chance of
selling even the good ones and have them
develop subsequent problems, we withdrew the
item from sale. This was a great disappointment
for the 493 fond grandparents who had ordered
Peruna and a great financial loss to Neiman-
Marcus, for in addition to having spent the

A million dollars is surprisingly hard to spend

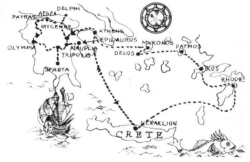

"P eruna" was built on a steel frame with a polyester and fiberglass body and was covered with a coat of silky-dyed sheepskin. He had a flowing white natural sheepskin mane and tail. Harnessed with a cowhide saddle and bridle, he turned right or left with just a flick of the reins. Most important of all, he was completely house-broken.

money for a full page we were still loaded with a herd of horses. We eventually gave them to orphanages around the country.

One of our customers from Minnesota came forth with a suggestion for the 1965 catalogue. She wrote, "Why don't you demonstrate how to spend a million dollars at Neiman-Marcus? I think it would make very good and interesting reading." We accepted the challenge and assigned one of our best-spending buyers to the task of how to make the beau geste of all time. She worked assiduously on the task, but she came up with $101,878.38 unspent.

We veered away from life's basic necessities, planted our feet firmly in mid-air, and selected luxuries—the rare and unique, the very precious. The list included a lace handkerchief for $300, a custom-made Black Willow mink coat for $75,000, a diamond necklace for $461,000 with a baguette diamond bracelet to match at $10,000, a crocodile tote bag for $1,500, a wardrobe of French kidskin gloves for $300, a dinner service for twelve in Flora Danica porcelain from Denmark, an original model of a Dorothy Doughty teapot, and a twenty-five-day pleasure party for ten on a chartered yacht that would sail through the Aegean Sea. There were other things included in the selections, but a million dollars is surprisingly hard to spend.

On one of my visits to New York, my good friend, that remarkable gourmet, bonhomme, and wine expert, Gregory Thomas, then president of Chanel Perfumes, invited me for

The "Things You Didn't Know You Needed Until Now" page showed a "Kocktail Crutch: For incapacitated elbow benders. Includes everything but the bar-maid: ashtray, place for glass, pillbox, little black book, even a key chain. Fifty-six inches tall, $20"; a whalebone bristle hair-brush at $8; and, shame-fully enough, a twenty-four-karat gold-plated "throne" seat for "His or Her" at $250.

luncheon. He advised me in advance that he was going to have a most unusual dish on the menu. My curiosity was heightened, and my mouth salivated for twenty-four hours till we met for luncheon at the Four Seasons restaurant. We didn't have to wait long, because the first dish was the surprise. It was "golden" caviar. I had seen all sorts of caviar, ranging from gray to black; but not only had I never seen "golden" caviar, I had never heard of it. It turned out that there was a limited supply of caviar of this color which had been previously reserved for the Tsar of Russia and the Shah of Iran. For the first time, a small supply had been allocated to the United States. I doubt if it actually tasted better than the best of Beluga caviar, but it certainly looked different. I located the agent who had imported it and reserved the balance of the supply for the 1965 catalogue. Here was exactly the type of news-making novelty that would satisfy not only the press but, even more important, our most discriminating customers. We photographed a Baccarat crystal caviar dish with fourteen ounces of "golden" caviar at the combined price of $130. As an alternative, for those who didn't like the idea of "golden" caviar, we offered the everyday ordinary top-quality Beluga gray caviar at $49.50 per fourteen-ounce tin.

Neiman-Marcus, Christmas 1966

the first day of Christmas my true love gave to me . . ."

"*B*e nice to your web-footed Gifts, that swan may be somebody's legend!" The sales promotion director began: "Most everyone is familiar with the lovely old English ballad, THE TWELVE DAYS OF CHRISTMAS, in which the lady love of an obviously smitten young troubadour acknowledges his daily offerings. She is so thrilled with her baubles that she never complains about having to cope with the size of the gifts and their multiplicity. Realistically, seven swans a-swimming might make grand alliteration and onomatopoeia but they could play pure hell with the plumbing.

"However, in this year of 1966, the problem is more HIS than HERS. Even if she could accommodate: twelve lords-a-leaping, eleven ladies dancing, ten pipers piping, nine drummers drumming, eight maids a-milking, seven swans a-swimming, six geese a-laying, five gold rings, four colly birds, three French hens, two turtle doves, and a partridge in a pear tree, could he afford his thoughtful and historic whimsy? Just what would the tab be to play this Twelve Day Game in hard American dollars?"

She ends up with the bad news: "This brings the grand total to $1771.50—subject, of course, to local, city, state, federal tax, sales tax, and tax tax. And none of it deductible, for him. And not much returnable, for her. Which is why this ballad remains a legendary verse."

*I*n 1966, our guest designer was the American artist Ben Shahn, who did a perfectly delightful cover that wrapped around front and back depicting the characters from the old English ballad "The Twelve Days of Christmas." To start off the catalogue with a bit of humor, we asked our sales promotion director, the inimitable Jane Trahey, to write an essay explaining the ballad.

In the inevitable frenzy that started the first of January and ended the day the catalogue was put to bed, we racked our brains for fresh and creative ideas for the "His and Her" pages. Dozens of ideas were considered and rejected until we zeroed in on the idea we thought might be the big one of the year. I had been reading about the period of Louis XIV and had come across an engraving of a double bathtub in which the King and his Queen or whoever else could enjoy bathing side-by-side. (This just goes to show that Neiman-Marcus didn't start the "His and Her" game; the Sun King beat us to it.) We took the idea to Crane and Company, who designed contemporary "His and Her" bathtubs, which we placed in the catalogue.

Shortly after publication, however, we received an official document from France stating that a bath shop in Paris claimed a copyright for the idea of the double bathtub. We turned it over to our lawyers, who discussed the matter at great length with the plaintiff's lawyers; finally the whole incident became so involved that I was advised by counsel not to

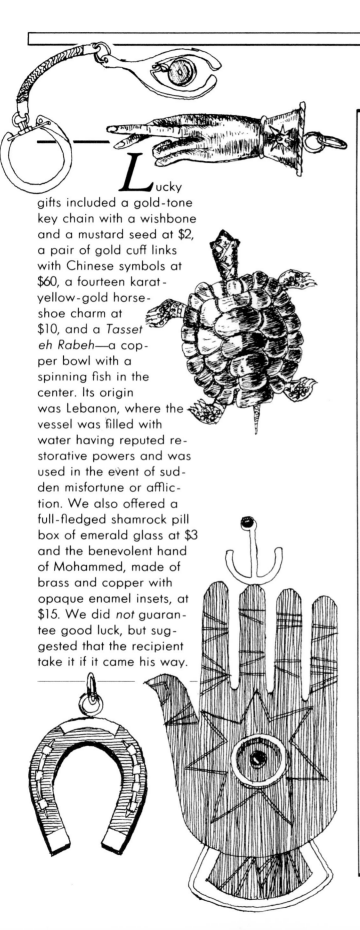

*L*ucky gifts included a gold-tone key chain with a wishbone and a mustard seed at $2, a pair of gold cuff links with Chinese symbols at $60, a fourteen karat-yellow-gold horse-shoe charm at $10, and a *Tasset eh Rabeh*—a copper bowl with a spinning fish in the center. Its origin was Lebanon, where the vessel was filled with water having reputed restorative powers and was used in the event of sudden misfortune or affliction. We also offered a full-fledged shamrock pill box of emerald glass at $3 and the benevolent hand of Mohammed, made of brass and copper with opaque enamel insets, at $15. We did *not* guarantee good luck, but suggested that the recipient take it if it came his way.

go to Paris on an annual buying trip lest I be arrested. We eventually settled the nuisance suit for a few hundred dollars, and I was thus free to resume my business affairs in France. This page, incidentally, reaped great publicity value all over the world, even before the suit was publicized.

In searching for catalogue ideas, I have frequently found inspiration from the sales techniques of members of the sales staff. We had an apparel saleswoman who had developed an enormous clientele in a very short period of time. I was curious to discover her selling secrets, so I watched her sell one day. I observed that on almost every sale this woman would tell the customer, "This is a very lucky color"; or, "This is a very lucky design"; or, "This dress has a very lucky button on it." I cautioned her about misrepresentation, for I doubted that she could prove that good luck would come to the customer who made the purchase. She replied, "I keep in close contact with my customers, and I can assure you that none of them have had bad luck."

Inspired by this bit of sales philosophy, we devoted a page to so-called "lucky" gifts.

One of the ways we built the Neiman-Marcus fur business into one of the largest fine fur operations in the country was by purchasing the finest bundles of skins sold at auction and by getting the first shot at new color mutations developed by leading breeders. We always had to pay premium prices, but we were invariably successful in finding customers who wanted the

unusual and were willing to pay for the privilege of being first.

In 1966 we were the top bidders at the Hudson's Bay Company auction for the darkest—in fact almost black—ranch mink skins that had ever been produced in commercial quantities. The prices we paid for these "Black Willow" mink were so high that many newspapers carried the story on their front pages. We photographed the pelts in the catalogue, stating that they would be made up into coats on special order at $75,000 for the number one bundle, $50,000 for the number two, and $35,000 for the number three. Before the book went to press we had sold both numbers one and three, leaving the middle bundle at $50,000 still available for purchase, which was so stated in the catalogue.

In early December a prominent customer from Oklahoma telephoned Doc Rowland, the dean of our fur-selling staff, to inquire if Doc had seen his wife looking at anything particular that he might consider giving her for Christmas. A few weeks later the same customer called back to say that his wife had put him in the doghouse for having gotten tight at a debutante party at the country club the previous night and he wanted a suggestion about what it might take to get him out. Doc asked if he had a copy of the Christmas catalogue. "Yes," the customer replied, "I've just been going through it." Doc said, "Look at page forty-six. I'll personally guarantee that this will get you out of the doghouse." The man reacted so loudly when he saw the $50,000 price tag that Doc thought he

Skiing days never end with your own ski slope in your back yard. This one is 121 feet long, 25 feet wide, and 25 feet high with SkiTrack plastic surface that skis like snow and no snow shoveling, $100,000 complete with lights for night skiing.

was in the next room. Then there was dead silence. Finally a subdued voice asked, "Do you know how she wants it made?" Doc assured him that he did know and that by coincidence he had his wife's measurements on file. All catalogue sales did not come through the mails; some came over the phone.

The handkerchief buyer had an idea of making pure silk chiffon scarfs into long-stemmed roses. We couldn't find a manufacturer who was interested in the project, so we made them in our own packaging department. They were finished off with florist tape and packed in a regular florist-style box with the traditional green tissue. A trio of these roses sold for $7.50. We didn't keep very accurate records of our labor costs, but we felt the idea was so charming that it shouldn't get lost just because of production difficulties. Our customers thought so too, for they had us manufacturing them right up to Christmas Eve.

That year not only did we have printer and supplier problems, but we had consistent ones with the U.S. Postal Service. The 1966 catalogue was printed in Chicago and was to have been mailed from the central post office. But a postal strike was in progress, forcing us to divert our catalogues from Chicago to neighboring towns where postal facilities were less clogged than in Chicago. As a result, some books were not delivered until November 20. This delay in delivery caused late orders and completely destroyed our order forecasting technique. We had record cancellations of almost 45,000 orders.

The Neiman-Marcus Christmas Book 1967

*S*ome of my zaniest ideas have come when flying across the ocean at thirty-five thousand feet, with no telephone calls or unexpected visitors to interrupt me. Such was the case in 1967, when I was racking my brain for the big gift for that year's catalogue. As I was thumbing through an Air France magazine, an article on camels caught my eye and I thought what silly-looking animals they were. I was reminded of the quip that camels weren't designed by the Lord but by a committee He had appointed. Suddenly, it occurred to me that "His and Her" camels would be a real laugh-provoking idea with enormous publicity potential.

When I returned to Dallas, I revealed my brainstorm to my colleagues, none of whom shared my enthusiasm. Some thought it was silly; others raised the kind of practical problems related to shipping and public liability that were designed to shoot down the idea. I pulled executive privilege as the boss and made the decision to use them.

The final selection of the "His and Her" feature gift was kept in great secrecy to prevent news leaks prior to the catalogue's publication. Information on the camels was so restricted that we didn't even notify the mail order operations manager; only when he saw the finished book did he become aware of the fact that he might eventually have to arrange delivery of one or more of these critters. Our research had located a camel supplier in

"*I* wonder who's   *the darn fool getting that?*"

Thousand Oaks, California, and had received a price quotation f.o.b., the ranch.

With that information we proceeded to photograph a pair for the catalogue. Not until we received a call a month before Christmas from Tom Barnett, vice-president of our Fort Worth store, who said that he had a sale for a lady camel, did we consider the practical problems of crating, shipping, and delivery. Although advertised as a pair, we saw no reason not to accommodate the customer who wanted just a single animal. After the purchase was confirmed, we dumped the problems of fulfillment on Don Shipman, our long-suffering operations manager.

He arranged for shipment, en route feeding and care, and final delivery to the recipient's residence. The camel arrived on Christmas Eve on board an American Airlines freighter about 8:30 P.M., in time for live coverage of her disembarkation on the ten o'clock TV news.

A woman in Fort Worth was sitting at home with her daughter watching the TV news that night. When the story broke and it was announced that the next day some lucky woman would find this camel under her Christmas tree, she turned to her daughter and said, "I wonder who's the darn fool getting that?" The next morning, she found out. It was under her outdoor Christmas tree.

I am happy to be able to report that this camel is still alive and is probably enjoying the good life to a greater extent than any other camel in the history of the world. The recipient

*T*he year 1967 wasn't just the year of the camel: we had another bombshell item. The catalogue showed a full-page picture of a demure girl in pigtails wearing a newly developed silvery nylon tricot short nightgown, which proved to have sensational sales appeal. At $28, it became the single biggest-selling article of feminine apparel that we had ever catalogued, producing over 9,000 orders.

*O*n our "Things" page, we gave readers the opportunity to lease a grapefruit tree in the Rio Grande Valley at a cost of $100 for the life of the tree, plus $5 per year for tree care. This entitled the lessee to all the grapefruit the tree could produce. There was a fourteen-karat-gold nail for a man to hang his hat on, an oversized package of "Silly Putty," and a lifesize inflatable vinyl figure of a man to sit along side a solo night driver for $5.

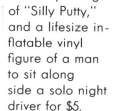

learned to love the camel and even bestowed her own name on it. She built special quarters for the beast on her estate and proudly exhibits her to visitors who come from far and near.

Another page was devoted to a collection of nineteenth-century enamel objects by Carl Fabergé (shown on page 115), a beaded *shahtoosh* robe for a woman at $2,795 (which was ordered by a Venezuelan for his wife's Christmas gift), and a turtleneck tuxedo shirt made of satin-striped cotton broadcloth.

Eddie and I had a bitter argument about the inclusion of this last garment. He was as much in favor of it as I was opposed to it. I thought it was in bad taste if worn anywhere but at a ski resort. He disagreed vigorously, and I yielded. He was right, for at $20 it became the single biggest-selling item in men's wear we had ever advertised. I still believe that we made a mistake in failing to state the appropriate locations for its use; but the public loved it, and men wore them everywhere. We filled 6,500 orders before Christmas and the balance of 2,500 in January.

Wigs were at the height of fashion in 1967, encouraging us to offer a fanciful twenty-four-karat-gold wig at $35,000 (shown on page 115). It weighed ten pounds, and the one purchaser, a TV star, made a good buy, for her investment is now worth over $70,000 in gold content alone.

*T*he

most explosive item
in the whole
catalogue,
surprisingly
enough, was
a Mason jar
full of mint-
flavored peas

Mint Peas

*B*y 1968, Robert Indiana's
"Love" design had become so popular that it
was even reproduced on a United States
postage stamp. The coloring of red, blue, and
green seemed to be ideal for a Christmas poster
or catalogue cover, since "Noel" had the same
number of letters as "Love." I went to see
Indiana at his studio in SoHo to ask if he
would do a Noel Christmas cover for us,
utilizing that idea.

His "Love" design, an oil painting, was used by New York's Museum of Modern Art in 1965 as a Christmas card. It was also, in a sense, the greatest victim of plagiarism in the history of contemporary art. Copied versions of the design in plastic, metal, wood, and paper flooded the market, but since Indiana had failed to copyright the design he was unable to defend his proprietary rights. Then when the U.S. Postal Service chose it for a stamp, "Love" became one of the world's most widely disseminated works of modern art. For that usage, he did receive the modest fee of $1,000.

When I offered to pay him for the "Noel" variation of "Love," he quickly assented, saying, "Most people would simply have done it without paying me anything."

That year we anticipated the trend of changing lifestyles with an emphasis on physical fitness. This was reflected in the catalogue, with a male jogger's outfit being presented along with a "His and Her" sauna.

In Italy our gift buyer came up with a stunning aquarium of contemporary design specially made to hold either salt water or fresh water. The art director let his enthusiasm run away with him by replacing sand with cultured pearls, resulting in a prime example of "overkill." We had a perfectly good idea which was made silly by the extravagance of pearls. This demonstrated how tight the editorial control of a magazine or a catalogue must be. With many capable people working on a project, there will always be a diversity of opinion.

*A*lso as a first in this catalogue was a page advertising a set of Martex bedsheets imprinted with jungle animals. It was called "The Lair" and showed a man and woman in bed together on and beneath the jungle sheets. We thought that there might be some kickback from some of our more conservative readers, but instead of kicking they simply ordered 5,415 sets of sheets.

The most explosive item in the whole catalogue, surprisingly enough, was shown on the $5 page: a Mason jar full of mint-flavored candy peas from Italy. Our candy buyer had had the confection made for us in a small town in southern Italy. She was quite confident it would be successful, but she was timid in her sales forecast. The mail order director predicted a sale of 23,000 jars, but the merchandise manager felt that was too optimistic. He finally approved an initial order for 15,000 units. The order was cabled to our Florence office; but when no acknowledgment came back, we telephoned the manager, who said, "We didn't take your telex seriously. We thought someone at the store was playing a joke on us. Don't you realize these mints are all rolled by hand?" We assured them that the order was bona fide *and to put it in work.*

After the first few days of catalogue distribution, it became apparent that we had a monster on our hands. The computer indicated that we would receive a minimum of 20,000 orders. The buyer then got on the phone and reached the manufacturer, who said that he would try to find a solution to this seemingly impossible task. By the next week, she had a telephone call from the mayor of the little village, who explained in passable English that the municipality he represented had undertaken the project and that he had mobilized all of the women and children to meet the requirements of this great and important American customer.

In the end, however, they were unsuccessful, and we were forced to turn to a New York manufacturer who had just started to produce the peas.

Nothing of similar magnitude had occurred in the Italian village since the Pope had paid a visit in the fifteenth century, and nothing has happened since to disturb the idyllic quality of communal life. I am told by those who have been there recently that at evening time in the local bar, as the men sip their glasses of vino, they reminisce about la crisi degli piselli.

There's an interesting footnote to this extraordinary merchandising success: this same item had been offered in a cardboard carton the year previously and had been a failure. The buyer, Evelyn Semos, had retained her faith in the selling potential of the idea and repacked the peas in Mason jars. Packaging thus proved to be the difference between failure and success.

A woman from Alaska wrote, "On the receipt of the bottle of peas from my niece, I put them in boiling water, and to my consternation I found that the peas had completely melted. This has never happened to me in the many years I have been cooking peas." We then realized that our ingenuity had not gone far enough. We had failed to make the package foolproof; so, in subsequent orders, we inserted a notice, "Taste before you boil."

The Neiman-Marcus
Christmas Book
1969

Antoni

*In 1969 we went back to Ib
Antoni in Copenhagen for that year's catalogue
cover, which we reproduced as a foldout with a
caricature of Santa Claus on the front with his
long white beard continuing onto the second
page encircling the neck, like a fox stole, of a
pretty damsel. The back page was devoted to
the presentation of the gift wraps, now priced at
$1 and $1.75. The Treasure Chest concept had*

been so difficult to accomplish with the prices of boxes rising yearly that it was dropped from the line. The Stack-Pac continued, although the problems of educating and inspiring the sales staff to sell them became increasingly difficult as our business expanded to branch stores.

In the mid-sixties, a new and interesting development was occurring in contemporary art based on optical illusions. The foremost leader in this new school of painting was Victor Vasarely, a Hungarian who had moved to Paris and there met with great success. I was intrigued with Vasarely's work; during my trip to Paris that year I talked to his agent, Denise René, the director of a successful gallery, who took me out to meet the painter at his country home. I showed him several previous Christmas catalogues and told him that I wanted to commission him to create a design for a woman's scarf. At first he didn't seem interested. He said he was not a fashion designer and didn't want to get into that kind of business. I then asked him whether he printed on paper, which I knew he did. He smiled and said, "Of course, I do reproduce a lot of my designs by silk screen on paper." Then I questioned, "What's the difference between printing on paper and printing on silk?" He laughed and replied, "Printing on silk is more difficult."

He looked through the catalogues I had given him and said, "Well, if I do it, why not make a positive and a negative; and then you will have a 'His and Her' item for your catalogue?" His designs, "Vega MC Negative"

*T*he "incomparable gifts" included a cashmere nightgown weighing twelve ounces in a new cloth called Pertoosh, woven by the master Italian weaving firm Agnona, at $125; a Baccarat mille-fleurs paperweight at $125; an antique Japanese cinnabar cabinet decorated with flowers of jade and semi-precious stones, mid-nineteenth century, at $3,500; a crocodile handbag with a concealed jewel tray at $575; a sixteen-piece set of mats and napkins, hand embroidered on organza in Madeira at $285; and caviar by the month, with a Baccarat crystal server that we guaranteed to refill each month for a year with a seven-ounce tin of giant-grained Beluga caviar from Iran at $600.

For those with less money to spend, there was a four-leaf clover etched on green glass, fourteen-ounce highballs at $10 for the set of eight, a large container of strawberry preserves at $8.50, and, of course, the familiar scissors knife at $5, now including three initials.

W e were very excited in 1969 about a new contraption offered to us that embodied the latest electronic developments. It was a remote-controlled golf caddy that would follow the golfer around the course at an obedient six- to eight-foot distance. It would operate for twenty-seven holes before the batteries needed recharging, and even folded up to fit in a standard car trunk. It retailed for $495; we thought it was sensational and catalogued it. Then the manufacturer encountered production difficulties, never delivered our order and, so far as I know, took the whole contraption off the market. We had to make refunds to over twenty-five purchasers who had sent in orders.

and "Positive," were taken to Switzerland, where they were printed in a limited edition of 150 pair. They were retailed at $750 for the two scarfs, making them the highest-priced scarfs that had ever been marketed. Now out-of-print, they are quoted by dealers at $2,000 for the pair.

The catalogue presentation of the scarfs brought forth orders from collectors from all over the world—Finland, Italy, Germany, Switzerland, England, France, Japan, and the U.S.A. Not only did we get publicity through the normal news channels, but we were able to attract the interest of several art publications as well, which for the first time carried stories about the Neiman-Marcus Christmas catalogue.

A newspaper article about Peruvian corn seeds—which grew to a height of fifteen to twenty feet—inspired us to devote a page to "fast growth." In addition to the one hundred Peruvian corn seeds for $4, we offered other alternatives. For example, we suggested a baby girl elephant from Thailand, "weaned, healthy, and of good family at $5,000, f.o.b., Dallas." For long-term growth, we suggested a Galápagos turtle from the Galápagos islands at $2,200, f.o.b., Dallas; supply was limited, however, to the two available turtles. For short-term fantastic growth, the obvious answer was gerbils at $35 for the pair. Five elephants were ordered by Hollywood personalities and one by a nightclub operator in Florida. The two turtles were snapped up immediately, but the gerbils proved to be a flop. Customers who wanted them could purchase them locally.

One of the hits of the catalogue was the brainchild of Edward Marcus, who suffered from indigestion and was a regular user of Gelusil. In the belief that there were thousands who had the same malady, he searched the country for old candy-vending machines as Gelusil dispensers. He was right, for we sold over 200 machines at $45 each.

When I was in Israel the previous year, I had seen some of the wonderful hand-embroidered robes, made and worn by Bedouin women. Their elaborate cross-stitched patterns were inspired by the designs the Crusaders had brought to the Holy Land in 1096. Many of the robes were in poor condition, but almost all of them had undamaged embroidered sections. We decided to salvage these good parts and mount them on French wool hostess robes, which we had to fabricate in

our alteration department since no manufacturer was interested in such a tedious assignment. No two were alike, and at $300 each
we had a complete sellout of the thirty-five
robes.

On page fifty-eight of this catalogue a
surprising face peeked out: Carol Channing, an
old friend and customer, had obligingly
accepted our invitation to be photographed in a
bed in between butterfly-printed sheets designed
by Hanae Mori, the Japanese couturiere.

Carol had discovered Neiman-Marcus
several years earlier when she was playing in
the Dallas Summer Musicals. She and her
husband, Charles Lowe, spent most of their
daytime hours shopping in the downtown store,
establishing close relationships in almost every
department with salespeople who acted as
personal mail order shoppers for them during
the balance of the year. Their warmth as people
and their loyalty as customers made them
beloved by the entire N–M staff.

On one of her previous Dallas visits she
had ordered 156 Christmas gifts for all members
of the cast and stage crew, to be delivered by
December 23 to Atlanta, where she was opening
in Hello, Dolly! on Christmas Day. Her husband
called in great distress on their arrival in
Atlanta to report that the gifts had not arrived.
We had specified special handling to our
gift-wrapping and shipping departments to
avoid any snafu on this important order, so we
had little difficulty in verifying that the
shipment had gone out on schedule. We were

*O*ne idea page was a "Petting Zoo." It was stocked with a pair of North American burros, New Zealand rabbits, goats, long-haired Shetland ponies, and domestic white ducks. This child-scaled zoo sold for $1,750. One of the several orders we received came from the purchaser of the lady camel—another surprise gift for her mother.

able to establish that the gifts had been delivered and that we had a receipt from the hotel's receiving dock, but the trail ended there. The hotel could not locate the carton.

I was notified about the situation on the morning of Christmas Eve, too late to duplicate the 156 specially wrapped gifts. The more I thought about it, the more I came to realize that the shipment had to be somewhere in the hotel. As I speculated about where it might be, I recalled that Carol was on a restricted diet and that her food was flown in from her home and put immediately on ice. I called Charles and asked if the usual instructions had been given to the hotel about handling her food. He replied that the food was there in the hotel's refrigerated vaults. "Go down yourself and I'll bet you $1,000 you'll find the Neiman-Marcus gifts there as well." Half an hour later he called to tell me that the hotel had put our shipment in the refrigerators thinking it was part of her food supply. Thus, a major mystery was solved, a customer satisfied, and a lifetime loyalty cemented. This incident may have been the reason Carol was willing to be our bedsheet model.

Another idea page showed a Honeywell kitchen computer which was programmed with recipes from Helen Corbitt's several best-selling cookbooks. Computers were at that point a novelty, and the idea of a personalized home computer was unheard of. This computer sold for $10,600, but it and its price were too far ahead of the times for salability.

Chapter 5
★
The SEVENTIES

*T*he postal inspector in Chicago shook his head; "We have more complaints on stolen Neiman-Marcus catalogues than all the other catalogues put together. When apartment dwellers see your Christmas books stacked in the lobbies, they steal them. Why don't you mail your catalogues in plain brown envelopes?"

This was a problem that Neiman-Marcus faced when its Christmas catalogues began generating nationwide attention; hence, the adoption of plain envelopes to diminish attention and reduce pilferage.

*T*he first catalogue we mailed in this manner was in 1970, a year of economic stress. A recession was in progress, and pessimism had spread throughout the land. I was on a coast-to-coast flight, and in the early hours of the trip I began speculating on the kind of gift that would best fit the gloom I had encountered on my visit to New York. It occurred to me that if we offered a gift suggestion for all of the pessimists I had run into, the most appropriate gift for them might be a Noah's Ark. That seemed to be about the height of pessimism. As the idea began to expand in my mind, it seemed to me that we should design a modern Noah's Ark and stock

the optimist...

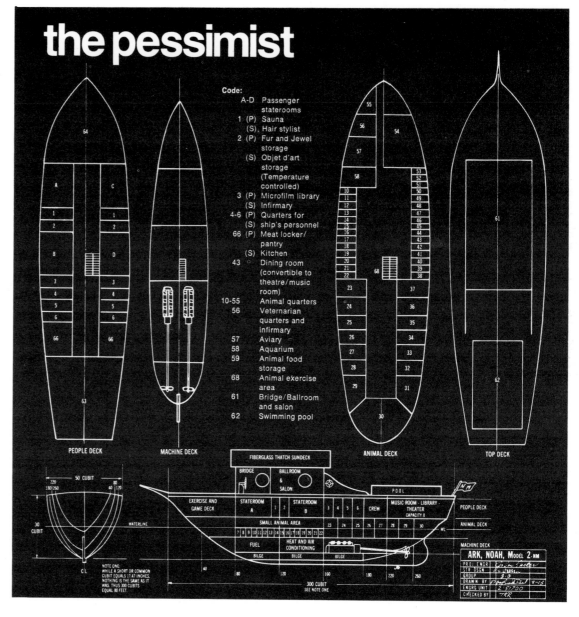

the pessimist

Code:

A-D   Passenger staterooms
1 (P) Sauna
   (S) Hair stylist
2 (P) Fur and Jewel storage
   (S) Objet d'art storage (Temperature controlled)
3 (P) Microfilm library
   (S) Infirmary
4-6 (P) Quarters for
   (S) ship's personnel
66 (P) Meat locker/pantry
   (S) Kitchen
43   Dining room (convertible to theatre/music room)
10-55 Animal quarters
56   Veterinarian quarters and infirmary
57   Aviary
58   Aquarium
59   Animal food storage
68   Animal exercise area
61   Bridge/Ballroom and salon
62   Swimming pool

PEOPLE DECK   MACHINE DECK   ANIMAL DECK   TOP DECK

ARK, NOAH, MODEL 2-NM

Is Ark a Lark?
'Perfect Retreat'
Costs $588,247

By MIKE BAXTER
Herald Staff Writer

Nieman-Marcus of Dallas, the department store that gave America-that-has-everything his 'n hers airplanes, has now offered Christmas shoppers the greatest calamity kit since Noah's Ark: the Ark, Noah, Model 2-NM, a bargain at $588,247 retail.

The store's new tongue-in-cash register Christmas catalog lists one drawback:

Delivery with mated animals — "endangered species given first priority" — requires four years, barring deluges and other major disasters.

For the impatient moneyed mariner, the store also provides a one-day Caribbean cruise aboard the T. S. Hanseatic "for you and 598 of your closest friends." Price: $35,000.

THE DALLAS STORE — make that mercantile institution — is so status-conscious that no dollar signs demean the price lists in the Christmas catalog. So, naturally, it would not really sell you a Noah's Ark. Would it?

"I pray every night that we will," said Edward Marcus, 61, chairman of the board.

He would rather sell a $10 tree, however. The catalog opens with the tree offer for "the optimist (who) takes the long view." The ark, advertised on the facing page, appeals to the pessimist planning "the perfect retreat from come-what-may."

THE ARK, a creation of store president Stanley Marcus, 65, Edward's brother, is a foreshortened version of the original — a common cubit equaled 17.47 inches in Noah's day, with such modern comforts as sauna and objet d'art storage.

The ark has attracted one serious offer, Marcus said. Not to buy, to crew. He said he had to reject a Canadian veterinarian's application. The ad clearly states a need for a Texas A & M veterinarian."

Then he admitted the ark is a complete fantasy, a catalog caper that has become a tradition at Nieman-Marcus.

The Hanseatic cruise is legitimate and not unconnected with the opening of a new Nieman-Marcus department store in Bal Harbour in January.

NEIMAN-
MARCUS
CHRISTMAS
BOOK
1970

*T*he cover
of the 1970 catalogue
celebrated the success
of the N-M logo,
which was offered in a
wide variety of merchan-
dise. There were white
coffee mugs printed with
brown N-Ms at $10 for a
set of four. There were
N-M plastic-coated play-
ing cards at $6.50 for two
decks and two score
pads. The graphics formed
the design of a gold-
plated metal compact at
$17.50; the design motif
was woven into the fabric
of a man's travel bag;
and, of course, there was
N-M gift-wrap paper in
the same design.

*it not only with pairs of all the species, but
bring it up to date by adding a French chef, a
Swedish masseur, a German hairstylist, an
English valet, an Irish maid, an Italian
couturier, an English librarian, a Park Avenue
physician, and a Texas A&M veterinarian.*

*Although the country was full of pessimists,
I realized there were still some optimists for
whom we would have to provide a gift, and that
perhaps the most optimistic gift one could give
would be an acorn from which a mighty oak
would grow. I took these two ideas back to
Dallas and talked them over with Tom
Alexander, our executive vice-president in
charge of marketing and sales promotion, who
liked the general idea but said, "Nobody could
be optimistic enough to give an acorn. Why not
offer an oak sapling instead?" So, we devoted a
double-page spread at the beginning of the
book—one labeled "The Optimist," with an oak
sapling that would grow to a height of thirty
feet or more at $10, and the other, "The
Pessimist," Noah's Ark stocked as I have
described it, at $588,247, f.o.b., Mount Ararat.
We cautioned prospective buyers to allow four
years for delivery of the Ark.*

*The result was most interesting: we didn't
receive a single order for Noah's Ark, but we
did get 1,561 orders for the sapling. All of which
obviously proves that there were more optimists
in the world than pessimists.*

*On the "Incomparable" pages, we repeated
the Vasarely scarf, of which we still had a few*

Our Lucite tub with built-in aquarium was the stuff myths are made of. It was 3 feet 2 inches wide (including 8-inch aquarium), 5 feet 6 inches long, and 18 inches tall. It arrived with fish and an Estée Lauder Youth Dew two-drawer beauty chest, $5,000 (plus shipping and installation).

Our linen buyer had come up with the wonderful idea of taking a client's favorite china pattern and repro-

ducing the design on hand-embroidered linen mats and napkins in the Madeira Islands. This was the kind of difficult-to-execute service that astonished new customers and pleased old ones who expected that kind of thing from Neiman-Marcus.

We were in constant search for luxurious new fibers. We had previously experienced tremendous success with vicuña, cashmere, and then the most marvelous of all of them, *shahtoosh*. We were excited to learn of a fiber that was unknown to us. It was the hair of the domesticated arctic musk-ox, which Eskimo women hand-knitted into scarfs and mufflers. An eight-and-one-half-foot-long scarf weighed less than four ounces and was priced at $150.

in stock. This time, we offered a single scarf framed at $425.

A double-page spread devoted to a custom-decorated room for children, which was to have been painted with giant animal murals by a well-known artist for $1,500, was charming, but turned out to be a complete flop as far as attracting any commissions.

However, the great surprise item in the catalogue and one that made news all over was the offer of a cruise "for you and 598 of your closest friends." For $35,000, the T.S. Hanseatic, *a cruise ship of the German-American Line, would sail from Port Everglades for an overnight trip through the Caribbean, with wine and food, dancing and games for the assembled company. Shortly after the issuance of the catalogue, we received a phone call from a woman in Miami, who said that her charity wanted to buy the cruise and that they would take the responsibility of reselling it.*

The
Fortress of the Freeway
was absolutely one of a
kind. This Total Transportation Security Environment
included the following
special features: **a.** anti-
theft device hood orna-
ment; **b.** closed-circuit
dual-lens infrared scan-
ning camera; **c.** infrared

periscope; **d.** 360° vision
indestructible cockpit bub-
ble; **e.** telephoto periscope; **f.** radar; **g.** dual-
exhaust antipollution
device; **h.** highway signal
markers; **i.** signals,
"Stop"—"Too Close";
j. marine prop; **k.** retract-
able tires; **l.** tank-tracks;
m. loudspeakers to warn
off passing motorists; **n.**
multilevel terrain stabilizer;
o. safety air bumpers; **p.**
padded safety bumpers.

*I*n 1971, our customer world
seemed to be divided between those who were
recalling with nostalgia their memories of the
good old days and those who couldn't wait to
get on the moon. We thought we'd poke fun at
both groups by opening with a double-page
spread entitled "Looking Backward/Looking
Forward."

We had great difficulty in finding a
backwards clock. The leading Swiss clock
makers told us it was impossible to make such
an instrument without retooling their factories.
We even tried the ingenious Japanese, who
failed us too. Finally, a local watch repairman

*F*or the backward-lookers, we offered a special performance of *No, No, Nanette,* with an after-theater party for all 1,244 guests, at a price of $42,-880. For those with permanent rear vision, we proposed a rose-colored rear-vision mirror for the car for $125 and a copy of the World Almanac, 1929 edition, for an accurate rereading of the past.

in Dallas constructed this masterpiece of time with no difficulty at all. It sold for $75.

For the forward-lookers, we had a wristwatch that gave lunar time, at $700. Most imaginative by far, however, was the Fortress of the Freeway, an exercise in total transportational security. It was, in a word, an $845,300 tank, payments being 10 percent down and the balance over thirty-six months. The idea was, of course, pure whimsy, published without any anticipation of orders. We were not disappointed; we didn't receive a single inquiry.

With rising prices, our buyers found so few gifts in the $5 and $10 category that they omitted this classification and concentrated on gifts "$20 and Under." To give you an idea of what was available in 1971 in that range of prices, we offered a hygrometer/barometer/thermometer in chrome at $15, a no-glue photo album bound in the cloth of a Japanese obi at $15, Imari patterned coffee mugs at four for $16.50, and a French coin purse made from genuine cobra at $15.

David Wolfe, our fur director, came up with the single biggest dollar-volume item of the catalogue and the numerically largest-selling "His and Her" idea we ever published. It was a blue jean jacket fully lined with natural brown sheared nutria at $275. We sold almost 500 pieces. The demand caught us and our maker by surprise, for no one could have forecast such a success story, particularly since the black and white photograph was not spectacularly good. It was a nice picture of the jacket, but it didn't

show the fur. This was a clear case of something selling from copy, which read, "OUR DENIM DE LUXE is fur-lined. For town, ski, or ranch, with button-out lining of natural brown sheared nutria." To keep up with the unexpected demand, our manufacturer's mother was taking jean jackets home to wash and bleach as late as two days before Christmas.

In this year's catalogue we included the presentation of Neiman-Marcus jewels, which normally had been produced in a separate, smaller-circulation catalogue. There were six pages of jewels printed in color, with photography, layout, and reproduction of a quality unsurpassed to this day. A big item was a 12-karat diamond ring for $150,000.

One of the biggest news producers of all times was our "His and Her" gift of 1971—"His and Her" mummy cases.

In 1969, when I was on a buying trip in London, I met a man at a cocktail party who told me that he had something that would make a fine feature for the catalogue. He owned an authentic mummy case, which he insisted that I see. I did take a look at it but explained that it really didn't fit into our merchandise plans. As I started to leave his flat, an idea occurred to me. "Is this a male or a female case?" I asked. He replied that it was a woman's case. "If you ever find a matching male case, let me know. We could feature it as a 'His and Her' gift." He replied with some disgust that he had no idea if he could ever locate one.

Two years later, I received a phone call

*O*n a lighter side, we introduced on the "Things" page a brass bobby-whistle from England and a mustache razor with a mustache comb at $7.75. Also included in that collection was a new bedsheet specially designed for Neiman-Marcus, the brainstorm of one of our merchandise managers. The sheet was printed with hundreds of lambs frolicking on meadowlike green splashes of color, obviously designed for our customers who suffered from insomnia. This was Neiman-Marcus's special way of making it easier for them to count their sheep. Sales exceeded even those of our "wild animals" sheet record-holder.

*from London. "Osborne here. I found him."
"You found who?" I inquired, having completely forgotten the whole incident. "I found a male case that goes perfectly with the woman's case you saw. Same period, same style." We made a deal on the phone, and I instructed him to ship them directly to Bal Harbour, Florida, where we had just opened a new store. A few weeks later I received a midnight call from the store manager. He told me that they had just received the cases, and when they had opened them they had discovered a mummy inside one of them. He wanted to know what to do.*

"Don't tell a soul until you get a doctor to examine the mummy and to give you a death certificate. We've inadvertently broken the law by transporting a corpse into the country, and we may be subject to a federal fine. We'll get our lawyers to appear before the customs authorities to admit that we unwittingly imported a mummy and throw ourselves on their mercy." Fortunately, the authorities understood the situation and on presentation of the death certificate passed the cases and the mummy. We gave the mummy to a local museum as a gift and exhibited the cases as planned.

The mummy cases made front-page news all over the world in newspapers and on TV and radio and were ultimately sold. I guess that proved we could sell almost anything. Nonetheless, we weren't sufficiently encouraged to open a mummy case department.

*T*he "In-
comparable" pages were
renamed "Superlatives,"
and under that identifica-
tion were placed such ar-
ticles as Hermès ties at
$18; a Han dynasty
bronze fishbowl, *circa* A.D.
200, at $1,750; a ninth-
century Japanese wood
sculpture at $8,500; a tiny
Fabergé hippopotamus of
pale green bowenite
with cabochon ruby eyes at
$6,000; and what we thought
was an eighteenth-century
Chinese snuff bottle made
from opal at $2,000.
Shortly after the catalogue
came out we received
protests from several au-
thorities claiming that our
dating was completely
wrong and that it dated
from the nineteenth cen-
tury instead. They were
correct—we had made an
error. We withdrew it from
sale since it was in dis-
pute, and subsequently we
did sell it for a lower price
as a nineteenth-century
object. As for the bronze
fishbowl, we received a
cable from a well-known
Japanese art dealer or-
dering it and instructing us
to ship it by air to Kyoto.
Three years later he sold
it to a Dallas real estate
tycoon for $12,000!

neiman-marcus christmas book, 1972

We commissioned a well-known artist to do the cover for the 1972 catalogue, but when it arrived it was so dull and unexciting that we were forced to reject it. We were caught at the last moment without a cover, and in desperation we utilized the Vasarely scarf that had been in the catalogue a couple of years previously. We still had a few of the scarfs on hand, and the Vasarely coloration and design made it perfectly suitable for a Christmas cover. It also helped us finally to sell off the balance of our stock.

1972 was also the year that I made the first of four trips to the People's Republic of China. I went over in the spring, immediately after President Nixon lifted the boycott on the importation of goods from the People's Republic of China. I was one of the first retailers to arrive in China.

My invitation to attend the merchandise fair in Canton arrived at the last moment, giving me little time to make any preparations. The officials extended entry cards for my wife and myself but no additional ones for our buyers. We arrived in Canton the day the fair opened and spent ten days viewing and buying the wares, which were scattered through several multistoried exhibition buildings. Purchases could be made from 9:30 A.M. until noon, and from 2:30 P.M. until 5:00 P.M. This was their first experience with American buyers, and our first with Chinese sellers.

I was able to
buy large collections of Chinese
Mandarin court robes, antique
porcelains, jewelry, and some
of the best of China's contemporary goods. In the catalogue
for that year, we featured a red
dragon court robe from the
Hsein Fêng period at $1,500
and a Celadon green porcelain
garden stool at $1,000.

Among a number of contem-
porary articles from China were
a tin of Ching Wo tea, rarely
exported from China, at $6
for two eight-ounce containers,
a table tennis set for $6, a gold-
washed silver cat lapel pin with
semiprecious greenstone eyes
at $20, and an acupuncture doll
(no needles) at $30.

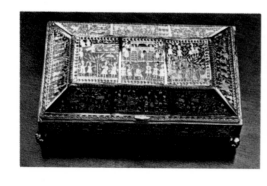

*O*n the less expensive side, we offered the Italian scissors knife, now $7 with three initials, a potted glass geranium plant from France at $7.50, and a marvelous dome ring combining rhinestones with green and brown enamel at an unbelievable price of $5.

Americans are accustomed to buying quickly without ceremony; the Chinese, on the other hand, were slow and deliberate with price quotations and information on the availability of merchandise. Their insistence that we drink tea constantly added to our frustration over trying to finish up our buying. Despite the fact that I was buying without the expert counsel of our experienced buyers, I purchased in that brief period over $1,000,000 worth of merchandise, which sold out within two weeks after its arrival in Texas.

Mr. Wong, one of the Chinese officials with whom we dealt, told a friend of mine who had accompanied us, Gerald Godfrey from Hong Kong, "Mr. Marcus is very nice man, but very stupid. He should have spent $5,000,000." Mr. Wong was probably right, but even when signing the contract for the mere million-dollar purchase I wondered whether I was in my right mind.

Acupuncture was very much discussed in America at that time, as was almost everything Chinese. After all, Americans had seen very little Chinese merchandise for a period of almost forty years. I found an acupuncture doll, sixteen inches in height, together with a book of instruction charts, which we catalogued at $30. When the catalogue came out, there was such a demand for the figures that we quickly sold out our supply. It happened that I was back in China in late November and received an urgent cable from the mail order director to buy 1,000 more acupuncture dolls. I checked with the

government warehouse, but it was too late to get anything from them, so I bought as many as I could from several of the Chinese Friendship department stores, lugged them as personal baggage to Hong Kong, and shipped them by air to Dallas to fill as many of the orders as we could. The profits from the sales were vitiated by the fact that I had to buy the last group at retail and air freight them.

The "Superlative" pages in 1972 included a pair of mid-nineteenth-century wooden carousel

AT WIT'S END

Life-Size Dummies Make Christmas Wish

By ERMA BOMBECK

Neiman-Marcus usually brings out a Christmas catalog with suggestions for the woman who has everything.

This year, they have a hot little item for the woman who has nothing. It's a life-sized model of a husband with a programmed tape recorder that keeps it saying what you want it to say.

They pointed out how for $3,000 you could order a life-size policeman for protection. Or a stand-in at the office. Or a busy person who wants to be two places at once.

If I'm going to sink $3,000 into a new live-in, I'm not going to fool around. I'm going to order me a Paul Newman who will pull me on his lap and say, "Turn off that stupid ball game, Bupie, and tell me again how much iron you take to stay so incredible."

At mealtime, I'll put Paul on automatic and he will assure me over and over again, "I didn't have this for lunch. I didn't. I never had this for lunch. No, never!"

My instant Paul Newman will never read the paper when I am telling him about the kids' retainers. He will never check the thermostat each evening to see if I have tampered with the seal he put on it. He will never get a hickey on his nose everytime I ask to use the car.

My new toy will take pride in carrying out the garbage, find humor in the fact that the screens are stored under the fire-wood left over from the year before, and never question why I added the rent to the balance instead of subtracting it.

He will never sit in the drive-way in the car laughing at a disk jockey when I wait dinner. He will never read in bed when I have lost my sunglasses. He will never offer to take me to dinner only when I have an impacted wisdom tooth.

As I told my husband, "I don't want to make you insecure or anything, but I am thinking of replacing you with a $3,000 dummy."

He turned the pages of his newspaper slowly. "What does it do for $3,000?"

"It will do or say anything I want it to."

"Can you get them in women's sizes," he asked.

"Sure. You could get one to ask you what kind of a day you had . . . or one to call you at the office and ask what time you are coming home. Or one who turns off the 11 o'clock news and tells you what happened to your son at school . . . or sits on the edge of the bathtub while you shave and tells you something is rattling in the car . . . or . . ."

"How much does one cost that doesn't do anything? You just jam it in a closet and it sits there and stares?"

---

horses from India. The pair, two feet long, were sold for $2,500. We had an elephant hide traveling kit for men at $100, "His and Her" miniature metal and lacquered bird cages from Japan, circa 1800, which we sold with a pair of rare pope cardinals, alive and colorful for $1,500. One of the most unusual things to be offered was a pair of giant Narwhal tusks mounted on pewter bases. These were quickly snapped up by a collector from New Orleans.

There were two idea pages that year, neither of which was very successful from the point of view of sales but which did generate good publicity. The first gift was "His and Her" lifesize dummies made to reproduce the image of anyone the buyer chose. (We had been inspired by a successful English play called Sleuth.) These dummies, operated by a remote control button that could be cued in to laugh at the most inane of jokes, could even be sent as proxies to sit in at a dull party. It proved not to be one of my best ideas.

The other big gift was one that Edward Marcus discovered. It was a jet-powered glider plane and it, too, flopped—for entirely different reasons. A beautifully designed craft, it held great appeal for those who liked to soar. The jet engine gave it greater mobility by allowing it to take off from almost any field and eliminating the necessity of a tow plane. But unfortunately the plane was never certified by the FAA, and while we had several responsible orders—at $32,000—we were unable to fulfill them.

*T*he 1973 catalogue, with a Bjorn Wiinblad cover, devoted its "Incomparable" pages to our imports from China. The antiques that I'd bought in the fall of '72 arrived in time to be presented in that year's catalogue.

Among the robes that I purchased, there were some that had damaged spots. We cut the bad parts away and took the remaining pieces of embroidery, still in fine condition, to the distinguished bag maker Judith Leiber. She worked the fragments into superb handbags, which we sold with great success. In Peking, I had found some old coral bracelets ornamented with gold-washed silver and enamel, which she used as handles for quilted leather bags. These incomparable evening bags sold for $395.

Our buyers were now traveling all over the world, scanning the markets of both Western Europe and the Far East in an effort to come up with interesting, exciting, and well-priced gift articles for our customers. The rigidity of American production methods made it increasingly difficult for us to specify those changes in style, detail, or quality that would increase our customer satisfaction. We were closer to the customer than the manufacturer was, and our experience could have helped improve domestic merchandise, but our suppliers' resistance to change forced us and other retailers to seek out suppliers in Europe and the Orient who could and would make merchandise to our specifications. It was

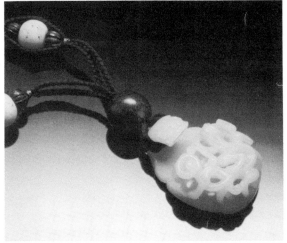

interesting to note that in the pages devoted to gifts of "$25 and Under," twenty-two out of thirty-two selections were directly imported from abroad. The remaining ten gifts were purchased from American manufacturers, but I suspect that in at least half the cases, they were acting as middle men for foreign factories.

Inexpensive items are also "order starters," for once the customer starts to fill in an order form there is greater likelihood that other items will be added. This technique is known as "overcoming customer inertia."

This year the press provided the lead to two of our idea pages. A story appeared in one of the newsmagazines about an industrial designer in Atlanta who was so concerned with the lack of privacy in our culture that he was designing rooms and capsules as retreats that would assure complete seclusion. This sounded interesting, so we commissioned him to design to our specifications a compartment which could be entered by the insertion of a special sterling punch card into the entry slot.

The other idea page was inspired by the news report of the controversy that arose when the Metropolitan Museum of Art in New York purchased a pair of Greek kraters for $1,000,000 under conditions of great mystery and alleged illegality. When I was in London, I came across some lesser Greek kraters at much more modest prices, and it seemed to me that we would capitalize on Tom Hoving's notoriety to garner publicity for ourselves, while simultaneously poking a little fun at the Metropolitan. We devoted a page reproducing "His and Her"

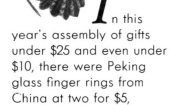

*I*n this year's assembly of gifts under $25 and even under $10, there were Peking glass finger rings from China at two for $5,

Fortnum and Mason breakfast tea in a small wooden chest at $6, a sterling silver thimble decorated with a band of pale green enamel from West Germany at $8, and a hummingbird lapel pin from England in golden metal set with rhinestones at $20.

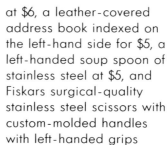

*G*ifts for left-handed people included a golf putter at $18, a left-handed golfer's glove for $7.50, a clear acrylic ruler with the numbers reading right to left at $6, a leather-covered address book indexed on the left-hand side for $5, a left-handed soup spoon of stainless steel at $5, and Fiskars surgical-quality stainless steel scissors with custom-molded handles with left-handed grips at $8.

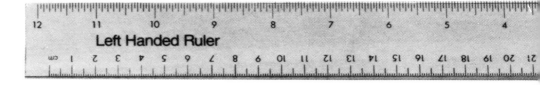

Left Handed Ruler

"Y_{ou} relax in an atmosphere psychologically fitted to help you accomplish peak mental and personal potential. Individual needs are determined after your in-depth interview with the designers. Colors, equipment, accessories are as variable as a person. Basically, whatever else goes into your World, the dimensions are twelve feet by fifteen feet, with sliding panels to permit a one-way view of either the actual outside world or superimposed film of your choice of location. There will be a lounge—your choice of chair, couch, waterbed, or cushions. Completely soundproofed from exterior noises, your World can be filled with sound—whether musical or of nature—that best unravels the paths of your mind." Since there were so many variables, we couldn't quote a fixed price. Instead, we stated, "The World begins at $85,-000." We had numerous inquiries and lots of publicity, but no sales.

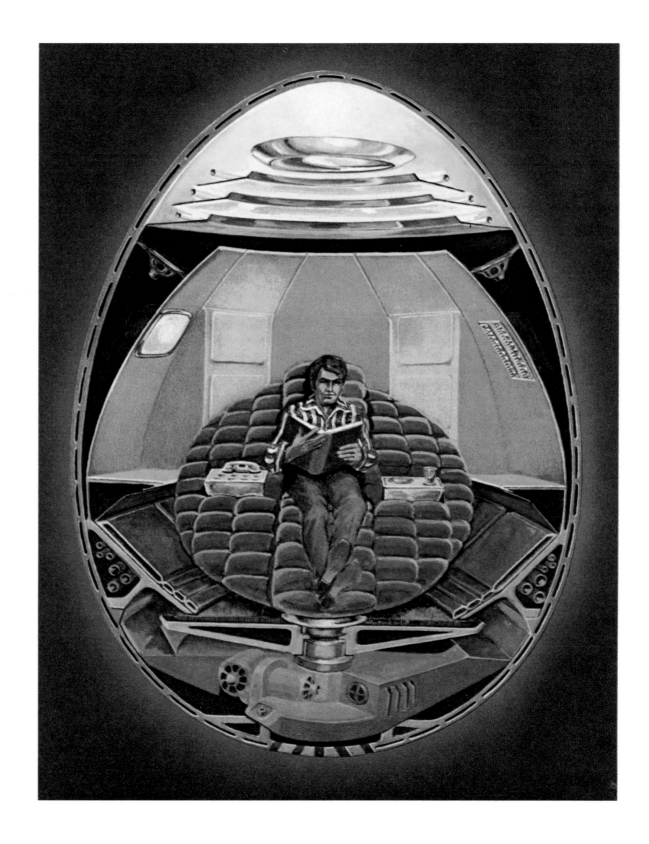

Greek kraters, about which we wrote: "There can be no controversy about these genuine Greek bell-kraters unearthed in southern Italy, dating from the mid-fourth century B.C. Not painted by Euphronios nor made by Euxitheos, these kraters have been authenticated by archaeologists and have been imported legally. No skullduggery or clandestine meetings were involved in their acquisition. Each pair will be accompanied by a certificate of authentication." We had acquired five pair of kraters, and we received orders for about twelve, priced at $5,000 for the pair.

Sometimes, creative efforts backfire. We had such an experience when an imaginative costume jewelry buyer conceived the idea of having a watch face made with Chinese characters instead of the usual Roman numerals. The characters were supposed to spell out a Chinese adage. We explained to our customers that the characters represented the twelve conditions an ancient emperor was given by the wise men to regain the lost love of his wife and daughter.

One day we received a complaint from a Chinese student that the real meaning was, "We shall take America over by force." When other authorities confirmed this translation, we immediately withdrew the watches from sale. We asked for an explanation from the manufacturer, who reported that one of his assistants had cut the characters from a Chinese newspaper and pasted them on the dial. Since Chinese characters express ideas

*N*o skullduggery or clandestine meetings were involved in the acquisition of our Greek kraters, dating from the mid-fourth century B.C.

"*S*ecure the future. Many of our customers have been turning to the purchase of unset diamonds as a very real investment in these somewhat unsettled financial times. The gift suggestion we offer on this page could well be the gift of a secure future for the recipient. It is just what you see—a bag of loose diamonds. Some are round, some pear-shaped, some marquise- or emerald-cut. To hold the diamonds, our special chamois bag with fourteen-karat-gold drawstring as an extra touch. The price of this precious cache of security will be of your designation, between $50,000 and $200,-000."

*F*or "Things They Didn't Know They Needed Until Now," we came up with a gold putter in the shape of a human foot for "the putter who makes one-foot putts" at $18, Mideastern wooden worry beads "to lift the tensions from your psyche" at $8, a Gordian knot puzzle of stainless steel and braided cord from the Design Centre in London at $25, and an English walking cane of polished wood, which lit up and blinked to illuminate the path on nocturnal strolls, at $37.50.

rather than exact words, many differing interpretations can be made from them. We still don't know whether the message was a deliberate propaganda attempt or an accident.

In 1973, we offered sound advice to our customers about investing in diamonds. A picture in our catalogue showed a leather pouch from which assorted shapes and sizes of diamonds were spilling forth. After publication, we received a complaint from a diamond dealer's wife, who claimed she had suggested this idea to us several years previously. We had no record of such a proposal but settled the matter by making a nominal purchase from the dealer. This sort of complaint is a constant hazard in cataloguing, for many times ideas do come in and get turned down by a buyer, only to be picked up a few years later by a new and completely innocent buyer who believed he had thought up an original idea.

On a flight to London, my wife called my attention to an article in the *Pan Am* magazine. It was a story about a little shop in London specializing in gifts for left-handed people. This is one minority group that has surely been ignored, I thought, so I made a visit to this dingy little store to see how they had solved the problems of lefties. We bought a few of their products and added several others, enabling us to present half a dozen gifts for left-handed people. Response to this page, while good, was not overwhelming enough to encourage us to open a permanent left-handed shop.

In 1974 we used a print by the Japanese-American artist Ay-o, done in his typical style of undulating bands of rainbow colors ranging from pale yellows to oranges, reds, purples, and greens for the cover. On the inside cover was a letter from the new President of Neiman-Marcus, my son Richard Marcus, welcoming both new and old readers to the 1974 catalogue. The frontispiece was the presentation of my first book, Minding the Store, *which had been published just a few months earlier. To my great satisfaction, the book became the best-seller of that year's catalogue.*

The "Superlative" pages continued the presentation of our importations from China, including a pair of very unusual robes, one of which was a twelve-symbol, silk, imperial yellow, sacrificial robe once worn by an emperor of China and which earlier had been exhibited in the Metropolitan Museum of Art. It was a K'o-ssu tapestry from the Ch'ien Lung period, circa 1770, at $6,000. The other was a donor's robe awarded to an honored civil officer of the highest rank. It was designed with white cranes within the mandarin square and had large calligraphic designs on the sleeves symbolizing single-mindedness and benevolent administration. It was embroidered in gold-wrapped silk thread and came from the K'ang Hsi period, circa 1700. It was priced at $7,000.

There were two idea pages. One was the N-Bar-M Mouse Ranch, a whimsical concept which reproduced in miniature the details of a

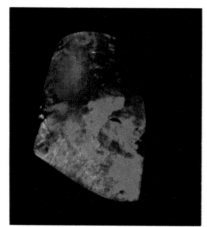

*T*here were more of the Judith Leiber one-of-a-kind evening bags at $450 and an antique lilac jade pendant carved in the form of a wild plum, hung on a necklace of agate beads, for $2,500. On other pages there were ties from Hermès at $23.50, handmade kidskin gloves from France lined in pure silk for $50, a muffler scarf of precious *shahtoosh* now advanced in price to $350, and a superb black boulder opal from Australia, of museum quality, weighing 106 karats, at $150,000.

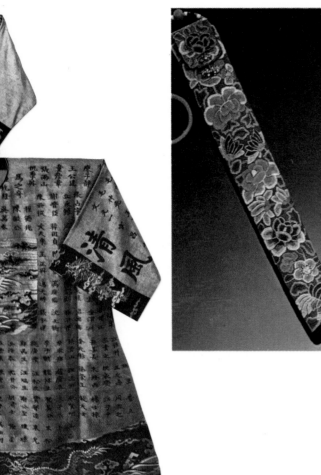

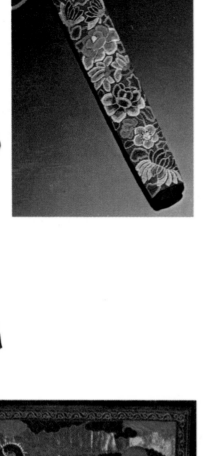

working ranch reduced to mouse scale, including feedlots, windmills, barns, and even mouse-size cactus. It was offered at $3,500. The other page featured "His and Her Hoverbugs" made by the Eglen Hovercraft Company. They were described as "Revolutionary two passenger crafts that move or hover on a cushion of air, six to eight inches off the ground—or water! Licensed as marine vehicles and conforming to Coast Guard specifications, the Hoverbugs move effortlessly from land to water, cruising at an average speed of thirty-five to forty-five mph depending on the surface you travel. HIS OR HER HOVERBUG, completely assembled with removable cockpit enclosure, carpeted and upholstered. Red or white, $3,640." These pages produced great international publicity but little business, although more customers were interested in Hoverbugs than mouse ranches.

Our gift buyer had found a superb nickel-plated brass penguin-shaped ice bucket on his trip to Italy. It was eighteen and one-half inches tall and was priced at $450. It seemed to me that we could get a little added humor and news value if we put something unusual into the ice bucket. Plain American ice obviously wouldn't have much news interest, so we got a price on a shipment of genuine iceberg ice from the South Pole. The penguin filled with South Polar ice went for $3,450. We sold a lot of penguins but I shudder to think of the problems had we been forced to call upon our ice man to fulfill a large number of South Pole ice orders.

Jogging suits for women and men were

*T*he silver jewelry boom was just starting, so we devoted a full-page spread to gifts in sterling silver priced from

$10 to $35. This, I think, was one of the finest color layouts that we ever succeeded in producing, and the sales results more than compensated for the space devoted to the presentation.

represented in a full-page photograph, which was a sure indication that the demand for such outfits was sharply rising. Western wear for men and women became more prominent in this catalogue, as did a wide variety of leisure clothes for both sun and ski resorts.

This catalogue marked the first time in the history of the Neiman-Marcus Christmas books that every page was in full color. From the standpoint of art direction, photography, and typographic design, I must rate this as probably the best catalogue that Neiman-Marcus had published up to this time.

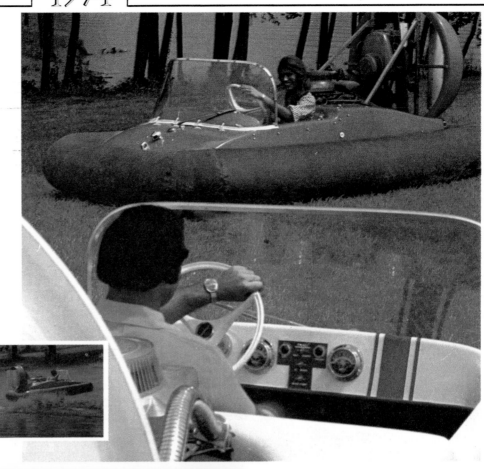

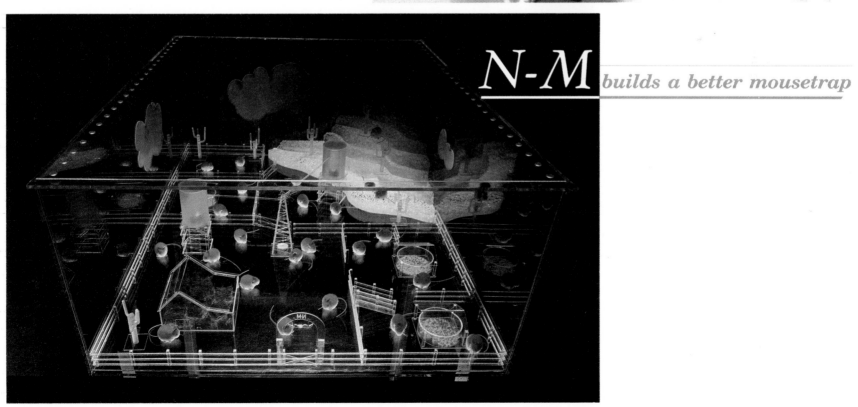

N-M *builds a better mousetrap*

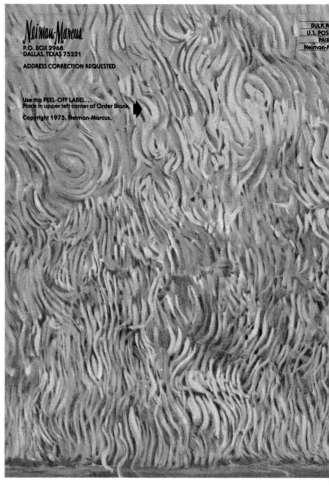

Giant carnivore found in Utah

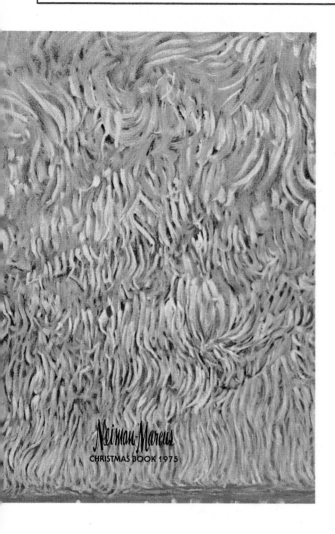

Neiman-Marcus
CHRISTMAS BOOK 1975

A *three-volume publication entitled* An American Portrait *was presented in an opening double-page spread of the 1975 catalogue. It contained a multiple sculpture and ten original graphic works numbered and signed by the artists, including works by Alexander Calder, Paul Jenkins, Henry Moore, Jesus Soto, and Mark Tobey, whose lithograph was selected to be the cover of the 1975 book.*

That year, we had the opportunity to acquire original letters by President Washington and his wife Martha, the authenticity and value of which we had verified by a leading Americana dealer. This made an ideal "His and Her" gift, and we presented them in leather portfolios at $9,500 for the set. These were purchased by an autograph dealer.

This was my first year of retirement from the store, and I had relinquished responsibility for the production of the annual catalogue. I thought the big gift idea was a sensational one. It involved a "Saurian Safari" or, in other words, "a paleontological safari into the wilds of east central Utah, to search for the remains of Allosaurus—the giant carnivorous dinosaur that preyed upon its more benign and vegetarian contemporaries." It was a ten-day safari, and came complete with a guarantee that a skeleton would be found for the purchaser—who, in turn, could give the skeleton to an accredited museum or similarly appropriate institution of his own choice. A

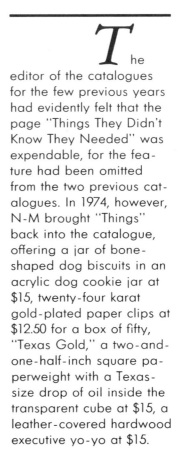

*T*he editor of the catalogues for the few previous years had evidently felt that the page "Things They Didn't Know They Needed" was expendable, for the feature had been omitted from the two previous catalogues. In 1974, however, N-M brought "Things" back into the catalogue, offering a jar of bone-shaped dog biscuits in an acrylic dog cookie jar at $15, twenty-four karat gold-plated paper clips at $12.50 for a box of fifty, "Texas Gold," a two-and-one-half-inch square paperweight with a Texas-size drop of oil inside the transparent cube at $15, a leather-covered hardwood executive yo-yo at $15.

bronze donor plaque to accompany the skeleton was supplied, as well as a bronze cast of the monster's skull for the hunter to keep as an indication of his contribution to archeological research. The safari, with one guaranteed Allosaurus, was priced at $29,995. Within a week's time after publication we had an order; but unfortunately, two months later, when it was time to pay for the purchase, the company buying it as a gift for its local museum was in financial difficulty and had to cancel the order. Fortunately for us, our deal with the supplier was subject to the buyer's prepayment. We were not required to keep an Allosaurus in stock.

We found an increasing acceptance of expensive articles of apparel in the catalogue, provided they were carefully and accurately portrayed. There was a dress made of twenty-seven separate scarfs at $250, which exhausted both our and the manufacturer's stocks. A tunic pants outfit imprinted with Japanese lanterns, at $295, resulted in similar sales.

A few years prior to this catalogue, I had designed a pipe when visiting an Italian pipe factory. I took a soft piece of stem and molded it in my fingers and asked the maker to bake it for me. He replied, "Che pazzía," meaning, "How crazy." I said, "Well, it's my money. Go ahead and bake it." He proceeded to do so, and I smoked the pipe on the rest of my trip through Europe. Everywhere I went, people wanted to know where I had gotten the pipe, so although I was now retired from N–M, I urged the

In the 1975 catalogue there was a page headed "Here Comes the N-M Gravy Train!" "Introducing the world's laziest Susan. Small talk won't be sidetracked while our sterling and silver plate, HO gauge waiter zips around the track to the call of 4 control switches delivering gravy, salt and pepper, condiments, sugar, and lemon. For dessert service or cocktails it could handle nuts, mints, olives, onions, and sauces. The hard working little engine is silver plate—a replica of those used in lumbering and mining. The four cars are sterling silver. The oval track has a polished walnut base, forty-four inches long and thirty inches wide, to blend with the best table settings. The engine and cars have their own velvet lined case to keep them safe and untarnished when the gravy train is not on duty. Special order, $8,000."

*O*fferings for "$25 and Under" in 1975 included a miniature bale-of-cotton package consisting of thirteen hand-rolled cotton men's handkerchiefs for $10, and a Sony AM-FM pocket-size radio at $22.

*I*n 1975 we offered the finest turntable in the world for $2,250. It was carefully constructed almost to eliminate residual noise levels and included a computerized digital display to monitor continuously the speed of the turntable, enabling unerring accuracy. We also offered a pen you could really count on—a compact calculator built into a reliable ballpoint pen for $80.

management to stock it and put it in the catalogue. The pipe had great success over the counter, and it was shown in the 1975 catalogue as "The Chairman's Pipe."

Also depicted was an all-time favorite of mine among the unique idea pages. It came from our vice-president Tom Alexander, who had read about an Indian rajah who had a miniature silver-plated railroad train made for his dining room table. Tom came up with the idea of reproducing it. I thought it was a brilliant idea, and I was delighted with the worldwide publicity that ensued from its publication. We had commissioned four sets and had sixteen requests, a few of which we were able to deliver as late as midyear.

In 1975, the toy buyer discovered a super Christmas gift for children, "The Moon Walk." It was an inflatable red, white, and pink plastic trampoline, thirty by thirty feet, with a domed plastic roof which made it completely safe for even the youngest of children. Among the twenty-six orders was one from J. Paul Getty, who on delivery refused to pay the transportation charges, although they were plainly stated in the catalogue. After repeated unsuccessful attempts to collect, I went to a Getty gasoline station, had my car filled with gasoline, and refused to pay the tax, referring the matter to Mr. Getty.

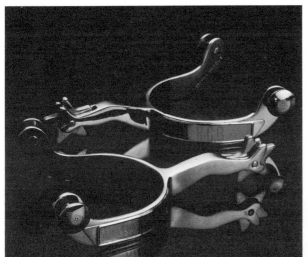

Give us a home for *our buffalo to roam*

Neiman-Marcus
CHRISTMAS BOOK 1976

*T*he 1976 idea page was a good one: "His and Her" buffaloes. It had been suggested by a rancher who had developed the first certified 100 percent purebred buffalo herd in the United States. We knew that the number of potential buyers for these animals was fairly limited, although several ranchers in the Southwest did end up purchasing them.

We offered a fine alternative gift for dude ranchers: a roll of forty uncirculated buffalo nickels in mint condition dated 1938—the last year the buffalo roamed—at $450. This idea unfortunately got scrambled into a page of other gifts, losing its significance and its full sales potential. Merchants call this a "throw-away" presentation—the kind of good idea that gets lost because of poor execution. Nearly every catalogue has at least one.

A polyester jersey, long-sleeved dinner dress broke all of our records for women's wear with sales of 5,800 pieces. "His and Her" stainless steel and brass and copper spurs and a pair of jumper cables in a Neiman-Marcus signature canvas bag closed the book, which had a cover, incidentally, of a mola designed especially for Neiman-Marcus and executed by the Cuna Indians in Panama.

Neiman-Marcus
CHRISTMAS BOOK 1977

Use this PEEL-OFF LABEL.
Place in upper left corner of Order Form.

©1977

Paul
Davis

*T*he 1977 catalogue was referred to as "the cat book," so named from the cover designed by Paul Davis, a well-known American illustrator. It showed a cat with a red bow and holly leaves tied around his neck. The picture became tremendously popular, both as a catalogue cover and as the design for the N–M shopping bag. To help differentiate it from the plethora of catalogues beginning to flood the mails, the catalogue was bumped up in size this

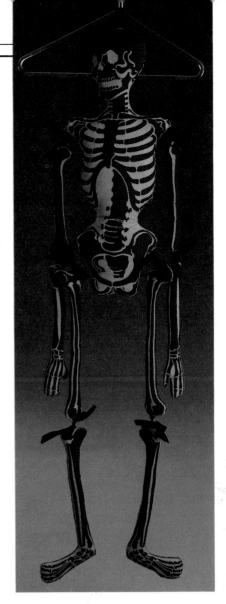

*O*nly 190 sets were originally made of this limited edition collector's cup and saucer, from a 1922 design by the great Russian/French artist Kandinsky. Cup and saucer in porcelain, $750.

year to nine and one-half by twelve inches.

Neiman-Marcus recognized the energy shortage by promoting "Urban Windmills," the big "His and Her" gift of the year. These were priced at $16,000 each, but they produced more publicity than orders.

We offered the most expensive lynx coat ever made from the prime bundles of Russian lynx sold at the Leningrad auctions in January, priced in 1977 at $130,000. One coat, one mail order!

We entered the field of fine art with a scarf printed on silk from a watercolor painting by Raoul Dufy, Le Yacht à Deauville. *Unfortunately, the copywriter was mixed up in her geography, for she wrote: "With pure color and unrestrained brushwork, Raoul Dufy painted into his sparkling* Le Yacht à Deauville *the very air of a warm Mediterranean afternoon." The scarf was priced at $180 in a limited edition of five hundred. As an add-on, the copy said, "The original watercolor, created in 1935, is thirteen and three quarter by twenty-four and three quarter inches, framed. $18,000.00." We received a mail order for that as well. Of course, Deauville is on the Atlantic Ocean and nowhere near the Mediterranean, as some hundred catalogue readers were quick to point out to us.*

We gave up the price category pages, which had proved so useful to customers, in favor of a section called "Gifts From A to Z." The change looked sensible on paper, but it actually made shopping more difficult for customers.

In the field of unusual suggestions, there

*T*o each of the individuals who wrote in, I sent the following reply:

Unfortunately, the copywriter for our Christmas catalogue is suffering from geographical delusions, a fact which we did not ascertain until she had mislocated Deauville to the Mediterranean coast. As punishment, we are sending her to Deauville for the months of January and February, where she will learn from firsthand experience that Deauville is nowhere near the Mediterranean.

Thanks for taking the time to set us right.

Sincerely,
Stanley Marcus

were two idea pages. We offered a seven-day expedition for five people into the heart of Lincoln Land. The trip, priced at $30,000, concluded with the commemorative planting of a red oak tree at the Lincoln farm. Although this didn't move, there was a complete sellout of a limited edition of Abraham Lincoln's poetry at $15. Another idea page was a charming one, I thought: a Neiman-Marcus Tree of the Month at $800 for twelve planted trees, but this met with only moderate success.

Unfortunately, most of the fashion subjects in the 1977 catalogue were photographed in the hazy atmosphere of the Rockies. The haze was so strong that it was difficult at times to identify the merchandise. But it was interesting as a recognition by N–M of the strong trend for western clothes for both men and women.

The title of the "Things" page utilized the same idea but was renamed "Worth a Thousand Words." There were several amusing items, one of which was an eleven-foot pole, the copy for which read, "Wouldn't touch it with a ten-foot pole? Try our eleven-foot aluminum pole. Collapsible. It comes packed in a black leatherette carrying case. $50.00." This was surely one of the cleverest ideas in many years. The other idea, my invention, was something that every family does or should have: a skeleton in the closet. It was four feet tall when completely assembled and retailed for $25. This skeleton proved a classic example of the problems a merchant faces in sales forecasting for a completely new product: we made 200 and could have sold 400.

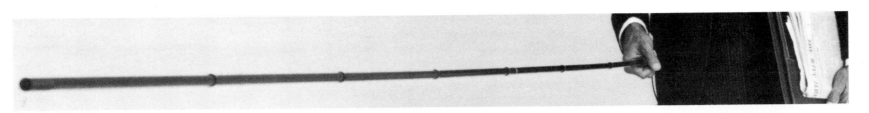

*T*he 1977 catalogue carried some interesting gift ideas: a gold-tone metal cat pin from England at $6; a pair of natural ranch mink ear muffs at $60; a set of six fourteen-ounce double old-fashioned glasses, half of which were engraved with "Joy," the other half with "Humbug"; a twenty-four karat gold-plated hard hat at $175; and a Zebra wood cigar humidor with a humidity gauge at $500.

Wile E. Coyote, designed by Chuck Jones, who originally created the character for the movies, adorned the cover of the 1978 book. The connection the coyote had with Christmas was hard to discern except for the fact that he was impaled on a weather vane and was going in a different direction from the silhouetted Santa Claus in his sled.

Parker Brothers, owners of the famous Monopoly game, gave special and, as I under-

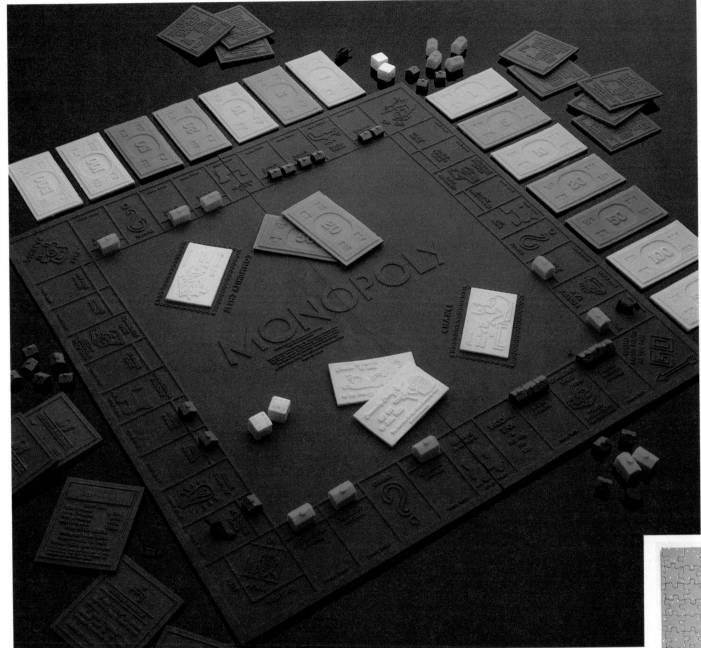

As appropriate tie-ins with the 1978 catalogue's cover, there were roadrunner and coyote lapel pins of gold-plated metal at $8. The scissors knife was back in at the now rapidly inflating price of $12. Tapestrylike cosmetic kits continued to sell at the higher price of $7.50. The very successful 1977 Paul Davis cat cover had been made into a jigsaw puzzle of a thousand pieces for $10.

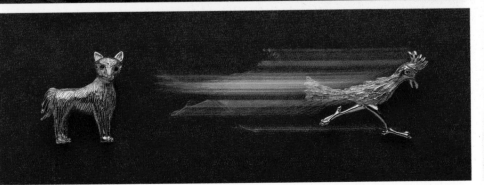

A page was devoted to the beautiful pre-Columbian replica jewelry produced by the Galeria Cano of Bogota using the lost-wax casting method. These authentic reproductions were photographed against the background of a Quimbaya terra-cotta figure. The pieces were priced variously from $28 to $225.

stand, the first permission ever to reproduce its game. An ingenious candy-maker from California by the name of Andra received approval to make a Monopoly set in chocolate and offered it to Neiman-Marcus exclusively for its catalogue. The set was run on the frontis-piece page at $600 and attracted worldwide comment, including an order from Hugh Hefner's daughter as a gift for her father. A year later, the National Geographic *magazine ran a story on Texas; in an effort to demonstrate the spirit of imagination that exists in the state, they photographed the chocolate extravagance in a full-color page.*

The western influence showed its growing momentum, in a white ermine-fringed western jacket by Ralph Lauren at $5,500. So successful had been the preceding year's lynx coat that a 1978 version was offered at $150,000. This was ordered by an eccentric lady in Rhode Island who was seventy-two years old. She wrote that she had always wanted a lynx coat and was specifying that she was to be buried in it.

Neiman-Marcus had some difficulty finding another big idea as a companion to the chocolate Monopoly page. The one they selected was less than inspired: a "His and Her" Natural Safety Deposit Box, one hundred and fifty feet long, located in the heart of a 9,000-foot granite mountain in Utah. It was esoteric, but not exotic; farfetched, but not fanciful. Apparently none of our readers was concerned about doomsday, for we had no serious inquiries.

Neiman-Marcus
CHRISTMAS BOOK
1979

*T*he last word in electronics was shown on the frontispiece of the 1979 catalogue in the form of a remote-controlled multisatellite antenna. As the copy described it, "The antenna directly points to the selected satellite in orbit above the equator, giving you choices from a staggering line-up of entertainment and information events to view from your armchair.

"With a flick of the switch you have options that include: over two thousand sports events yearly, six thousand hours of special children's programming, ten thousand top movies, live nightclub shows from Las Vegas and New York, sessions of the U.S. House of Representatives, a direct line to news agencies and business reports, the new super stations, and much more. All of this for $36,500." All you needed in addition to the money for the dream satellite was the time to use it.

One of the most entrancing ideas in the catalogue was the service of a pair of master chimney sweeps, Dee and David, who not only would do a professional job of cleaning your chimneys, but would put on a rollicking song and dance show in chimney sweep costume as well. As a corollary gift, Dee and David had created "The Dusty Doll" in a costume reproducing their own, at $27.50, as well as a children's book, Dusty the Chimney Sweep, at $8.50.

*P*ull the world to your doorstep
with the first remote-controlled, multi-satellite antenna

For the "His and Her" gift we pronounced, "This year, rise above it all with our 'His and Her' dirigibles." The ships were 120 feet long, powered by a seventy-two-horsepower engine, and would cruise leisurely at twenty-five miles per hour. The price was $50,000. Inquiries continued to come in as late as the fall of 1980. One of the first responses came from a ten-year-old boy, who found that we had not provided sufficient information on the specifications of the dirigible. He wrote a letter and included his own sketch with notations of both questions and suggested improvements.

*D*ear Sir:

I am ten years old and I read your add about your Dirigibles and am very interested in your Dirigibles, how ever there are some questions that I would like answered. I have inclosed my drawing of the questions I would like answered before I will think of buying your Dirigible. If I deside to buy your Dirigible, my grandpa and I will half to put our money together.

I plan to get a paper route and already have a saving account. I know that if all these answeres are alright grandpa and I will buy this dirigible. I will await your answer.

Sincerely,

*W*e answered:

Thank you for your recent letter inquiring about the dirigibles featured in our 1979 Christmas Book.

In answer to your questions, the dirigible is not self-inflating, as it is a hot-air dirigible operated in a similar fashion to hot-air balloons. The anchor rope is included, but I regret that there is no emergency potty on board. The passenger compartment is semi-enclosed and is large enough for two people, plus a well-stocked picnic basket. There is no antenna on the dirigible, but I think a small radio receiver could probably be carried in the passenger compartment.

I appreciate your questions about our dirigible, and if I can assist you any further, don't hesitate to contact me.

Sincerely,

*I*n a more down-to-earth vein were a set of six steak knives with black pakka wood handles for $25 and wooden zebras, about four and one-half inches in length, carved of Mvu-vuvu wood by the people of the Akamba tribe of central Kenya, a set of three for $50. There were also some amusing new ideas and some extravagant ones.

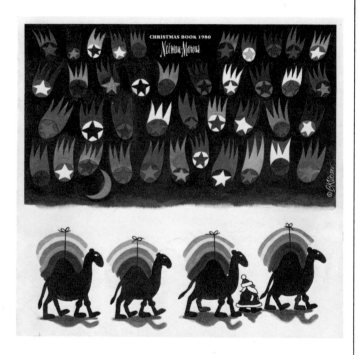

The catalogue for 1980 set a record, both for the dimensions of the book and for the number distributed. It measured eleven inches square, a change from the more traditional, rectangular magazine proportions of previous years. The circulation surpassed 1,250,000 for the first time. It took thirty years to grow from the 50,000 distribution of 1950.

The art direction and typography were probably the best that Neiman-Marcus has ever achieved, with the possible exception of 1974. Typographical aberrations that had marred the two preceding years' catalogues were corrected, making the catalogue easier to read and to order from. This has to be a primary consideration of cataloguing, as well as any other printed form of advertising.

Our ostrich offer (opposite) was attacked by conservationists and bird lovers with vehemence. The Washington Post reported the complaints, as did the wire services. It will be a long time before Neiman-Marcus ventures into a wild-life gift again—perhaps it will take another generation of management!

The crystal pages were particularly well photographed. Glass in general is one of the most difficult materials to reproduce photographically. A stunning cranberry glass vase, eleven inches tall, sold for $40, but looked like it might have been $250. Customers reacted to this excellent value and ordered more than a thousand of them.

The "His and Her" gift of 1980 was a pair of baby ostriches, the copy for which read: "Ecology is nothing to put your head in the sand about. Ostriches don't. Give a foster home to an engaging pair of young ostriches, and enjoy the fun of raising these gracefully gangly birds until they're ready to add to the collection of your favorite zoo or wildlife park. For all their strength, speed, and hardiness, these huge flightless birds are rapidly disappearing from their last natural habitats in Africa. If you have the room, keep them with you and build a 'herd' of your own. They love ranch life. At the rate of about thirty to forty eggs a year (each equal to about twenty-three grade A large hen eggs), it won't take long to count heads of ostriches. Meanwhile, you can: have one-egg omelet parties, gather the plumes that shed for decoration, stage impromptu ostrich races, learn the original Watusi dance derived from their flamboyant courting ritual, revive quill pens for writing, study their fascinating semaphore language, watch the insect population decrease, or convert the eggs into decorative items. Your pair of young ostriches (similar to those shown in the large photograph) will be hatched in the spring of 1981, a joint project of the Oklahoma City Zoo and the Monastery of the Holy Protection of the Blessed Virgin Mary. Your gift of this pair will be announced by a certificate. A pair of ostriches, $1,500." For those who either couldn't afford or didn't want a pair of ostriches, we offered a genuine empty ostrich egg for $35.

While there were a couple of pages of "Superlatives" at the beginning of the book, the items selected were surpassed by some of the objects scattered throughout the book. They showed a Rand McNally Geo-Physical Earth Globe, three feet in diameter, one inch being equal to 221 miles. This was a marvelous gift, but the scale of the photograph made it appear small, which obviously prevented the globe from becoming a more successful item. At $14,500, it was the kind of gift that might be given to a retiring corporate president or purchased by a chief executive officer for the lobby of his headquarters. The silver-plated roast beef cart from Cristofle of France at $24,000 was extravagantly priced, or perhaps it would be fairer to say it was priced beyond the point of real value.

The frontispiece showed a commissioned recording of original Christmas songs by two Dallas songwriters. We sold 4,018 of this two-record album at $19.50. A noble attempt to provide unique gifts was a one-of-a-kind Martin D-45 guitar made of aged Brazilian rosewood at $9,500, for which two orders arrived simultaneously. The vice-president of mail-order operations tossed a coin to determine the recipient. There was also a specially printed, limited edition of Coronado's Children *by the famous Texas folklorist J. Frank Dobie, designed by one of America's outstanding printers, Andrew Hoyem, at the Arion Press in San Francisco. Bound in Mexican bark paper with a goatskin spine, it was priced at $700.*

*T*he first year we went to a truly exotic place to photograph our catalogue was 1980. The Caryatid Gallery in the Park Güell in Barcelona proved a striking setting for a magnificent natural fisher coat from Fendi. Equally striking was the setting for the "Texas Star" dress designed by Michaele Vollbracht, an abstraction in black and silver bugle beads and sequins.

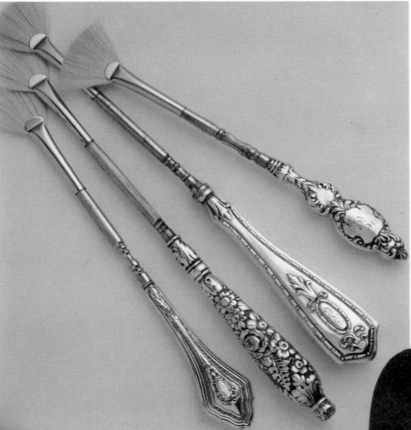

The "A to Z" formula of the two previous years was replaced in 1980 by the more traditional price classification "$25 and Under," a clear acknowledgment that this latter presentation meets the unspoken questions of the customers better than "A to Z."

There were some fresh and interesting items in this price range, including a wardrobe of three regimental-stripe stretch belts at $13.50 and chocolate truffles in a silvery metal basket at $11.

Not as inexpensive, but certainly beautiful, were makeup brushes with antique silver handles at $75 each.

CHRISTMAS BOOK 1981
Neiman-Marcus

*T*he Walt Disney
Christmas card used on the cover of the 1981
catalogue had a heart-warming spirit as it
depicted the familiar Disney characters, Mickey
and Minnie Mouse, Clarabelle Cow, Horace
Horsecollar, and Pluto, venting Christmas
gaiety as they are pulled through the snow in
an old-fashioned stagecoach by an antlered
horse past a milestone to another holiday

What's better than a third hand, more fun than computer games, gives the word "portable" a new meaning, was born to serve, and will do almost anything you want without demanding a day off? ▷▷

◁ ComRo I, the Domestic Robot System, by Ultimation, Inc., exclusively for Neiman-Marcus. ComRo I brings elegance to the computer age and a light side to the science of electronics. ComRo I will uncomplainingly open doors, serve guests, take out trash, bring in the paper, sweep, fetch, do light hauling, water the plants, dust, pick up after children (and pets), caddy at the putting green, walk the dog—and a host of other tasks and missions.

The standard model is a 4½-foot-high acrylic unit with spotlight, 300-foot-range wireless telephone, smoke alarm, fire extinguisher, vacuum, carpet sweeper, cigarette lighter, tote pocket, tray rack, utility wagon, scooper, squeegee, running lights, digital clock, black and white TV, extendable arm/hand manipulator, and a microcomputer. It operates on 12-volt sealed rechargeable batteries and will work like a demon for two hours continuously under normal usage (if it doesn't have to do windows). $15,000.

To keep ComRo I from being lonely, there's also the robot pet, "Wires." By radio control, it shakes its head, wags its tail, lights up, and blinks, squeaks, and generates amusement. "Wires," complete with carry case, is $650.

celebration. Mounted on a true Christmas red background, this cover, more so than many previous ones, proclaimed, "A Merry Christmas."

In 1981 the book contained something for everyone—and everyone's pocketbook—with gifts from $8.50 to $157,000.

One thing I never learned in my years as a retail merchant was why customers found music boxes so fascinating. But they do, and I have had to accept this fact as a matter of faith without trying to ferret out the reasons. The 1981 book featured a charming, nostalgic ceramic figure of Father Christmas mounted on a base holding a music box that plays, "Santa Claus Is Coming to Town," which, at $50, outsold any music box in the catalogue's history even though it was double the price of any of its predecessors. It is fair to conclude that though times may change, music boxes go on forever! I still don't understand.

There was a marvelous soft-sculpture barn for toddlers, filled with animals for $20; American caviar (for the first time) at $150 for a fourteen-ounce tin; a charming melon-shaped ceramic pitcher from France for $20; a marble lazy Susan for cheese at $30; and an amusing black sheep at $275 for families that don't already have one.

Red River pipes, smoking tobacco, and cigars were added to the Red River western line of outdoor clothes and ranch-type foods. The Helen Corbitt Collection, a posthumous book with 512 pages of favorite recipes, made its debut.

*S*omething for everyone

The "totally tame menagerie" by Steiff of Germany at $1,000 was delightfully presented in a color page. Each of the individual animals could be purchased separately. The white and brown bear with a red vest proved to be the real winner, though there were half a dozen orders for the complete petting zoo, including one from the embassy of an iron curtain country.

The big idea page represented the gift everyone would like to get: a "His and Her" robot. The press went to town on this marvel of the electronic age. Orders came from all over the United States and abroad, some twenty-eight in total.

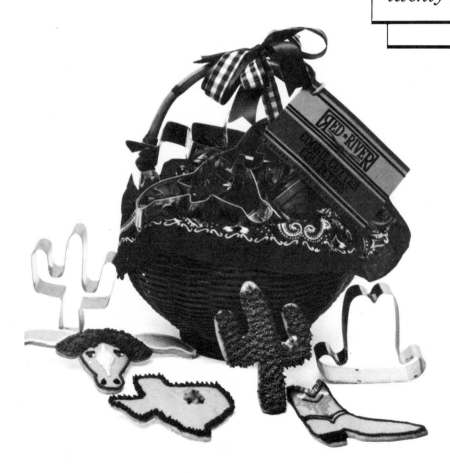

★
The FUTURE of & CATA- LOGUING

*I*n 1966, in a speech at the dedication of the School of Business at Indiana University, I forecast a marketing revolution to come which, for want of a better name, I called "phonovision." I said:

> The mass use of color phonovision will introduce a completely new dimension to remote buying and selling. In addition to mail order shopping, customers will be able to call their favorite local or out-of-town stores on the phone and see the articles over the monitor that will interest them right in the comfort of their own living rooms. The stores will provide shopping guides with sample smells to enable the shopper to make buying decisions with the same assurance either two or two thousand miles away from the selling floor. The salespeople will be able to tempt new customers with new products via phonovision instead of making the present-day inquiry, "Why don't you come in and see our new things?" After the decision is made, the customer will put her plastic card in the special telephone slot, and the salescheck will be automatically recorded at the store. Her account will be charged, or a cash payment will be made by a simultaneous telephone withdrawal of the amount from her bank account.

That was written fifteen years ago when my non-electronic mind was startled by this radical new possibility.

Now the revolution is beginning to arrive on the outskirts of marketing, and it may be that the printed glossy catalogue will be outmoded within a decade. Cable television is already here for more than a quarter of U.S. households. More than 2,500,000 homes and offices have video cassette recorders, with the probability of 4,000,000 by late 1982. Video disc players are selling briskly, and home computers, even at $1,200 and up, are becoming commonplace.

We're also seeing the beginnings of a software explosion, particularly the development of specialized programming, called narrow casting, to provide software

N-M invariably receives complaints, but surely the most gracious complaint of the season came from a lady in California, who wrote:

When I received the blouse I ordered from your wonderful Christmas catalogue, as a present to myself, I could hardly wait to open the package. I slit the tightly-wrapped paper, removed the gift paper, pulled back the tissue, and found a live bug on the front of the blouse. I love the blouse but I am returning the bug (dead). This is the first of three blouses I ordered, and I sincerely hope I do not receive any more bugs.

Merry Christmas,

To which I replied:

Dear Madam:
Although I am now retired from Neiman-Marcus, I am still keenly interested in the store's successes and failures. Neiman-Marcus has made its share of mistakes in the filling of orders; but to my knowledge, this is the first time the company has ever succeeded in delivering a *live* bug with merchandise ordered by mail. By the law of averages, I seriously doubt if you'll ever receive another bug from Neiman-Marcus—dead *or* alive. However, I am recommending to the management that they enlist the aid of that electronic marvel, ComRo I, shown on page 21 of the catalogue to help prevent any repetitions.

Sincerely,
Stanley Marcus

for all the hardware being marketed. This software will be to the mass market entertainment vehicles of broadcast television what Psychology Today, Road and Track, and Golf Digest are to Reader's Digest and Time magazine. This means it's becoming possible to reach people through video who have special interests, who are in particular income brackets, who are members of senior management, or who are workers on night shifts.

Advertisers and advertising agencies have had an increasing presence at the cable television conventions, but most of those attending have been from the media buying, entertainment, or programming side. They've been investigating the cost efficiency of video presentations that can target the smaller and more specialized audiences of 110-channel cable television systems for the several million well-heeled owners of video cassette recorders. There are opportunities for producing good informational narrow-cast programs that can serve as extraordinary marketing vehicles for many manufacturers and direct marketers.

Cataloguers face increasing problems as costs of production, paper, and postage continue to rise. So far, they've been able to absorb these costs without sacrificing profitability; but the time will come when the cataloguer will be forced to find more economical methods of communication and, at the same time, more responsive ones. It's ironic that just as the potential market appears to be expanding and just as it is the time for expanded direct mail efforts, costs of printing direct marketing are preventing expansion. The new technologies can prove to be cost-efficient solutions to some of these problems by the end of the decade.

Television sets are the second most widely distributed piece of hardware in American homes and one of the most adaptable. Television sets can be adapted to receive 110-channel cable systems hooked into telephone wiring for video text distribution, plugged into a home computer, or attached to a video cassette recorder or a video disc player. Together with an 800 telephone number, it becomes an instant response vehicle.

The most widely distributed piece of hardware in

American homes is the telephone. Since I made that speech on phonovision in 1966, push-button telephones have been taught to do all sorts of tricks, and many already function effectively as computers. The video phone, first demonstrated to the public at the 1938 World's Fair, coupled with the computer technology of the 1980s, is a superb information distributor. The primary reason the two-way video phone has failed so dismally in past tests has been that Aunt Susie didn't like getting caught at 2:00 p.m. with her hair still in curlers, and Uncle Richard couldn't bear being projected at 10:00 a.m. still in bed and nursing a hangover.

It's entirely probable that the Christmas catalogue of the nineties will be distributed either on video cassettes to be played at home, or at mini-electronic centers, or through catalogues specially produced for cable TV, with its immediate response through remote control.

By way of explanation, the direct response technique involves a hand-held key pad that can operate by some remote control through which it is possible to respond instantly to cast a vote or to buy a product without the necessity of writing out an order form or of phoning in a mailing address.

The individual elements of transmission, hardware, and distribution can be combined in a myriad of ways to enable any system to become interactive. Any and all of the systems I've discussed can be turned into interactive systems within a few years if, for instance, AT&T is permitted to forge ahead with information distribution to consumers. Any and all of the systems can have the equivalent of one-button-punch 800 numbers with all the credit and mailing information already programmed in at the head of the system.

One should not view these predictions with alarm. They should be accepted with the good grace that all new technological developments deserve. If and when they do come about, the public mail shoppers will find that they will serve them better than the catalogues of today. In the meantime, hold on to your catalogues, for they may well become the heirlooms of tomorrow.